YULE NEVER WALK ALONE

ALONE
25 Festive Reflections

Kate Williams

Book Layout © 2017 BookDesignTemplates.com

Yule Never Walk Alone / Kate Williams. -- 1st ed.
ISBN 979-8-3299519-1-2

"The Word became flesh and pitched his tent among us."
John 1:14

#YuleNeverWalkAlone

INTRODUCTION

Festive greetings! Thank you so much for buying a copy of this book. I wanted to start by telling you a little about the 'why' behind this advent devotional.

Christmas is one of my favourite times of the year - it begins early for me so I can milk it to the max! As soon as Bonfire Night (the 5th of November here in the UK) is over I feel like it's fair game to flip into full-on festive mode.

I love the Christmas tunes (*Last Christmas*, *Fairytale of New York*, and *Mary's Boy Child* are a few of my faves). I love watching Strictly on Saturday nights, with all the glitz and glitter. I love giving and receiving gifts, visiting Christmas markets and drinking Baileys hot chocolate and mulled wine. I embrace the fluff of the festivities and I definitely embrace the Quality Street tin (get your grubby mitts off the strawberry creams - they are my faves!).

I love watching Christmas films - *The Muppet Christmas Carol* and *The Holiday* are my top two (hey Jude!). I also love the lower budget films, so I get the Christmas 24 channel on and watch more Hallmark Christmas films than I'd like to admit to! My favourite is the one where the city girl (called Carol) moves to the small town on assignment to shut down the Christmas tree farm. She has a revelation of the magic of Christmas and quickly ditches her corporate boyfriend Chad as she falls in love with Hank, the humble and charming owner of said tree farm. It was 'love at first bite' of the (calorie free) gingerbread cookies they baked together, playfully dusting each other's faces with icing sugar - oh what festive merriment. After a brief falling out when Hank realises Carol came to town to shut him down, they quickly move on and save the tree farm, celebrating their success on an ice-skating date after the local Christmas pageant where they swigged back eggnog and sweetly sang carols. If you've never seen a Hallmark film you needn't waste time watching one now as that literally describes the plot of every one of them!

Whilst they are a bit of a sweet escape and a guilty pleasure for me, I recognise they are full of cheeseball cliches and sickly-sweet storylines that don't reflect real life. Most of our lives, and our experiences of Yuletide, do not resemble a Hallmark film in any way, shape, or form. Real, non-Hallmark life is a weird mix of challenges, fun, boredom, stress, blessings, irritation, rewards, excitement, and discouragement. I don't know about you, but I do not spend my December days baking and icing festive cookies, swigging hot chocolate next to a perfect man who thinks the sun shines out of my perfectly toned and tiny Hallmark hiney. If I as much as sniff any festive baked goods I put 3lbs on. My relationships, marriage, job, family, and friendships have ups and downs. My faith is strong, then weak, and then somewhere in-between. I can feel like I'm thriving in life and feel like a complete failure in the space of two hours. I'm not swanning around with a Hallmark grin and a perfect life. I'm sure that's not your reality either. (If you are swanning round with a Hallmark grin and a perfect life, please don't swan down my street - especially my Quality Street!)

Putting the corny Christmas idea of Hallmark to one side, if something valuable (e.g. a piece of jewellery or other things made from precious metal) has a 'hallmark', this means it has a sign of purity and authenticity. The hallmark details the maker's name. Because of Jesus, your ordinary life can actually have a heavenly hallmark. This doesn't mean your life will resemble a Hallmark movie - probably quite the opposite in honesty, the bible is clear that the Christian life is costly. But it means it's possible to live an authentic and pure life, walking with God, your maker, who sees your incredible value. He will help you navigate every challenge you face and celebrate with you in every moment of joy. I believe that a life given to God and stamped with his heavenly hallmark is the best way to live.

Aside from the Hallmark cheese and festive fluff I admittedly enjoy, as a Christian Christmas has a profoundly important meaning for me. It's the time where I remember that Jesus chose to come to earth. "The Word became flesh and pitched his tent among us" (John 1:14). Jesus' name is 'Immanuel' which means 'God with us.' Pause and reflect on that incredible truth. God is with us. God chose to come down and live among us. God understands the difficulties we experience because he too has experienced them. You will never walk alone. Or if you'd care to indulge in my festive pun, and the title of this very book, *Yule never walk alone*. Because that's the true meaning of this Christmas season - in Jesus, our Immanuel, we have a saviour who is ever present in the highs and lows of our complex lives on earth.

Over the next twenty-five days we will walk together through this exciting time of advent, when we anticipate the coming of Christ and celebrate the birth of the Messiah. I will share my reflections on various Christmas themes from personal experiences throughout the last few years. Some are light and I hope they make you smile. Some are a bit raw, and I hope they help you know that you aren't alone in your struggles and in the imperfection of your life. You may really connect to some of the experiences I share, or you may have entirely different challenges to me. The most important thread to reflect on throughout this devotional is that Jesus came down to live on earth, and because of this you have a friend and saviour who walks with you through your ordinary and imperfect life.

There's a beautiful video by an organisation called Speak Life that you can find on YouTube - search for 'He came down, special needs nativity.' I strongly encourage you to watch it - the following quote is from that video:

He came to our darkness from heaven above
He stooped to the crib and the cross out of love
He shared in our weakness and meekness and mess
And still he embraced us nevertheless
If you're feeling rejected, excluded, a stranger
Remember the one who came down to the manger.

He came down. He loves you deeply. He is Immanuel - God with us. Because of Jesus, Yule never walk alone.

Love Kate x

CONTENTS

1st DECEMBER – PIGS IN BLANKETS

Isaiah 40:11 – "He tends to his flock like a shepherd, he gathers the lambs in his arms and carries them close to his heart."

Now it's the first of December I feel it's fair game to start dreaming about the roast dinner that is to come - 24 days and counting! We rarely take the time to cook roast dinners in our house these days (sooooo much washing up involved!), but Christmas is a time when we make the effort and go all out for the Christmas dinner. When I say 'we make an effort' what I mean is that my husband makes the effort to cook what I refer to as 'the roast with the most.' However, I'm no passive by-stander, I'm a very diligent cleaner, table setter and sprout peeler/chopper so I feel I have significant input into the festive feast. My favourite elements of the Christmas dinner are the roast potatoes, bread sauce and pigs in blankets - mouthwater-ing.

Side note - my husband once tried to compliment me with what he thought was a festive term of endearment - he said to me "you're my little pig in a blanket." All I'll say is I wouldn't advise you to ever try this line. He had an all-expenses paid weekend in the dog house - no blankets provided!

Anyway! I used to work for a charity who were big on fes-tive fun. One year they asked us to decorate our departments with a Christmas theme, and our team decided to deck our department as a giant Christmas dinner. Our manager made a papier-mâché turkey, we suspended hundreds of sprouts from the ceiling, and enjoyed cheekily asking colleagues "do your sprouts hang low?" as often as we could. We all wore pig masks and wrapped ourselves in blankets. We came in the top three, pipped to the post by a team who pretty much built a stable and had a dog in the office dressed as a donkey. A fair but grudging loss!

I love eating pigs in blankets, but, like our team's life-size Christmas dinner, I also love this cosy season of being wrapped up in a blanket myself. My daughter loves this even more than I do! Particularly at the end of the day, she loves to be reclining on my knee with a blanket covering her, all cosy and snuggly. My daughter is seven, she has Down Syndrome, and communication is difficult for her at times. She signs well and her speech is coming on, but there are times she gets frustrated as she can't communicate what she wants or needs. Yesterday I was washing up when she came into the kitchen and both said and signed "mamma, big cuddle." She'd never said this before, and it was lovely to hear her communicate exactly what she wanted. I knew I had approximately three seconds to abandon the washing up and get under a blanket with her pronto before a hissy fit began! One of my favourite parts of each day is being cuddled up with her, looking at her gorgeous little chops, singing songs together and sniffing her soft hair - magical moments. (Apart from the windy times when she looks up at me and grins after letting off a stink bomb - no festive spiced candle can mask that smell!)

Yesterday I was doing my devotional reading and was encouraged to imagine myself curled up like a child in my

Heavenly Father's lap. It reminded me of the intimacy and love I experience with my daughter during our blanket snuggles. Our Heavenly Father wants to have these moments of us just being with him. Relaxing and reclining in his presence. Not asking for our list of things we need, but just experiencing and enjoying the closeness of our relationship with him. Being held by him and being aware of his great love for us. Not needing to perform or impress, just *being*. Often my daughter and I spend time snuggled up in silence, but we are very much communicating, even if not via speech. Even during our sometimes silent snuggles we are communicating our relaxed, unhurried, natural and comfortable connection. We are deepening our relationship. She feels safe, loved and secure, and I just love the quality time being close with my precious girl.

I feel challenged in this busy world, and in the inevitable craziness of the upcoming festivities, to take more time to just be with my Heavenly Father. I'm pretty good at remembering to talk to him each day - I often bring things that are on my mind to him. But I'm not good at just stopping and enjoying his presence. Acknowledging that I'm safe, secure, and I'm his beloved child. I don't often find the time to be still before him and to listen to him and receive what he has to whisper to me in the quieter, unhurried moments.

Throughout this festive season, despite all the busyness that's often ramped up beyond the normal chaos, could we decide to take the time to truly *be* with him? I think if we do, we'll have a deeper experience of his love this Christmas.

YNWA - Sum up and Reflect:

Your Father God longs for an intimate relationship where you spend time just being with him, enjoying and resting in his presence and growing in your understanding of how loved you are as his child.

Try your best to make time amidst all the crazy to be still before him and let him remind you how loved you are.

Do you regularly spend time with your Father God, just resting in him and acknowledging his great love for you?

If not, how could you build this into your day, even if it's just for 5-10 minutes to start with?

If it doesn't come easy, start by just finding a quiet space, maybe light a candle, focus on the flame and try to focus your thoughts on God's deep love for you.

Perhaps you could spend five minutes meditating on this scripture from Zephaniah 3:17: "The LORD your God is with you, he is mighty to save. He will take great delight in you, he will quiet you with his love, he will rejoice over you with singing."

Prayer:

Heavenly Father, I thank you for your limitless love for me. Thank you that I am your beloved child. You long for me to spend time with you. It's hard for me to grasp this and I'm often so busy that I forget to spend quality time with you. I know that if I take time to truly be with you and to reflect on your deep love for me, I will live differently. I know it will cause me to love myself and to love others around me so much better. I acknowledge that times of silence and stillness before you can be so beneficial and help me to carry the awareness of my worth as your beloved child into my daily life and into each challenge I'm currently facing. Please gently remind me to set aside time with you when I often forget amidst the busyness and demands of life. Thank you for the verse from Isaiah that reminds me that you are a shepherd who wants to hold me close to your heart, help me to choose to make this posture a priority each day. Amen.

2nd DECEMBER – O COME LET US A'DOOR HIM

Proverbs 19:21 - "Many are the plans in a person's heart, but it's the Lord's purpose that prevails."

After a spot of Google research I have significantly increased my knowledge on the origin of the advent calendar, and feel like I should be awarded an honorary degree in 'adventology' if you will! I can now reliably (well reliably-ish, depends on how reliable you think Google is) inform you that advent calendars began in Germany in the 19th century, when families would count down to Christmas by making marks on doors or walls. I'm not massively keen on the thought of marks on my lovely sparkly wallpaper, so I'm glad calendars have evolved since then! It developed into lighting candles or putting up a religious picture each day on the run up to Christmas. A German printer called Gerhard Lang started designing cardboard advent calendars and came up with the idea of cutting out little doors to open each day. Behind each door a bible verse or devotional picture would be hidden. Over the years this has snowballed (good festive analogy!) and chocolate companies have stuffed little festive chocs behind each door.

Although they started out with a very spiritual meaning, that's not really the case nowadays, but I'm not complaining about my 'secular' Malteser one - especially as I'll get a mini Malteser reindeer on Christmas Eve!

My advent calendar research has got me thinking about the theme of doors, and has caused me to reflect on a time in my life when every door seemed to open, almost as easily as I rip open my Malteser calendar door, stab the foil and grab the chocolate each day. This was early on in my marriage, and it just felt like there was a real ease to life. Everything just seemed to go smoothly - if I applied for a job I got it. If we saw a house we loved, it all went to plan. Ministries we were involved in really flourished and it all seemed pretty dreamy. We certainly worked hard in these areas, and were prayerful in all we did. Things didn't just fall into our laps by any means, but it really felt like every door we pushed opened with little effort. Like I could just blow gently and a door would fling open. I thought that this was what life as a Christian would always be like. If I trusted God and wanted to walk in his will, why would he not fling wide every door that was in front of me so I could skip through it happily singing 'shine Jesus shine' as I leapt over the threshold?! This 'open door' season lasted for quite a few years, then suddenly everything seemed to change! Doors suddenly kept shutting in mine and my husband's faces. We would apply for jobs, jobs that really fit our passion and gifting, and it was no after no after no. Disappointment, discouragement, rejection. I found this really difficult at first, as I had thought life as a believer might always be a bit of a breeze. Why would a good God who is on my side allow all of these rejections and let these doors slam so firmly in my face? But I have learnt to look at doors differently, and I now try to view a closed door as positively as a wide-open door.

Naturally, I think we all love an open door. I think this is because there's usually something exciting behind them - in terms of our advent calendars it might be a chocolate, a joke, or if you are very posh (oh jolly hockey sticks) even a mini bottle of gin. Open doors in life might mean a relocation, a new job, a new relationship, or a new home.

But we don't like the shut doors quite so much. They mean no new and exciting step forward: we don't get the job, the house move falls through. Life stays the same, but then often feels more mundane than ever. However, I believe we need to grow to a level of maturity where we thank God for the shut door as much as we do for the open one. We can absolutely mourn the closed door, but we need to try to see it as an act of God's kindness and providence, rather than rejection. God may be at work in closing a door in order to redirect us to the absolute best path for our lives. It's not really a rejection, it's actually a divine redirection.

I remember once applying for a job that I wanted *so much* and being *so gutted* when the door was shut. The difficulty was that the door was so close to opening as I got down to the final two applicants. I didn't get the job, but the people who interviewed me were so complimentary, and one of them said they really believed I would work for them in the future. I tried three times to get a job with this organisation and it just didn't happen. I know I had the right skills and the right passion for the roles, but I can see that even though my motivation was good, it was not where God wanted me to be. I can only see this now with the perspective of being five years down the line and knowing the job I now have is the best fit for me and positions me so well for the future job I have in my heart.

It was very difficult to understand that this was actually God's goodness and guidance when I was applying unsuccessfully while being so passionate about the work. I remember asking for prayer from a mature Christian who said they felt I needed to submit the situation to God and give up the desire to work there, and he could redirect me if he really wanted me there. I did try to pray along these lines, grudgingly at first (in honesty I was expecting a 'let's barge down the door in faith' style prayer ministry session), but as time went on I genuinely did give it to God and I did submit to his will. I resisted the urge to try to force the door, which can be so tempting. Eventually the desire to work for that organisation did leave, and I took myself off the email alerts for jobs with them! I know what I am doing now is right where God wants me to be and on reflection I'm so thankful for his closed doors and his redirection. However, I'm not pretending this is easy at all. There were a few years that followed my closed door that were exceptionally challenging. I had to knuckle down and commit to trusting that God would open the next door for me in his timing - and I had to do that through a period of redundancy shortly followed by the Covid-19 pandemic which meant I was unemployed for nearly two years!

I have learnt that if God is in something you can't stop it, and if he's not then there's no point trying to force the door. I take great comfort and confidence in knowing that no plan of His can be "thwarted" (Job 42:2). This means that nothing can stand in opposition to God's plan for you - if he's planned it, nothing can prevent it.

God's plans for you will be fulfilled. Remember that he has the big picture and knows the route you need to take to get you there. Don't stress and feel rejected when a door closes or remains closed. Mourn the loss if you need to, but do your best to thank God in faith for the shut door, and cling to the belief that 'there's more in store through a different door!'

YNWA - Sum up and Reflect:

Thank God for the doors he holds open for you, but also thank him for the ones he shuts - it's the Lord's good purpose that will prevail. He walks with you through the open doors and redirects you round the closed ones. He's got you. His plans are the best and he can be trusted.

The route you take towards his plans may not feel particularly nice. At times it might even feel discouraging and frustrating - that's certainly been part of my experience. But he is with you, and he will get you where you need to be through whichever doors are required.

Is there a door that has recently shut for you? Bring this to God now, along with all of the confusion, sadness, and disappointment involved in it. Ask him to help you to hold on to trust in his good plan, even though as it stands you may see no good reason for the shut door. Ask him to help you choose to believe he has reasons you know nothing about, and that ultimately it's for your good – because he has other plans in store that he can see but you currently can't. It's often as we look back on our lives in hindsight that we are actually thankful that God shut a door, even if it was a door that at one point we desperately wanted to fling wide open.

As you open each door of your advent calendar this year, say the scripture we opened with from Proverbs. No door can remain shut if he has planned for you to walk through it.

Prayer:

Thank you, Lord, for the doors you have opened in my life so far: when things change and open up for me, and I feel I'm able to step forward into new and exciting opportunities. However, I want to grow to a level of maturity where I also thank you for the doors that close. I want to be able to acknowledge it's painful when doors I have prayed to fling wide are shut, yet maintain a deep trust that it's because you have a different plan. Thank you for the scripture for today that says your purpose prevails. Walk with me and comfort me in the disappointment of closed doors, but give me that spark of hope and excitement to believe that you have a different and a better course ahead for me.

3rd DECEMBER – I'M A CELEBRITY GET ME OUT OF HEEEEEERE

Proverbs 4:23 - "Above all else, guard your heart, for everything you do flows from it."

I'm a Celebrity... is on in the UK every November, hosted by the two cheeky Geordie chappies Ant and Dec. When it finishes it means that Christmas is nearly upon us and full-on Christmas mode is activated - even though I'll have been watching Hallmark Christmas films since bonfire night! I'm a Celeb is not a programme we always watch, but this year (I'm writing this reflection at the end of 2023) we have watched a lot of it! It's not been as dramatic as other series have been, there have been few fall outs and very little bad behaviour. (Obviously I only like to see such things so I can pray for those involved, not because it makes for good TV). I was curious to watch it as the former health secretary Matt Hancock was appearing in it, and I couldn't quite believe that was happening! During the Covid-19 pandemic he was a controversial character, as he was leading many of the daily briefings telling us the rules we should follow to keep everyone safe and well. It transpired that he broke his own rules, and he was caught on camera snogging a woman who wasn't his wife. People were rightly outraged and disappointed that someone who should have modelled the correct behaviour was doing the exact opposite.

Sadly, this is often reflected in the lives of Christians, and this year there have been so many Christian leaders particularly who have 'fallen from grace' and behaved in a way that is the opposite of what they stand up and preach each week. It makes me really sad when this happens. Sad for them personally, sad for their families, and sad for their congregations who have looked to them for leadership and guidance. It's so disappointing when someone we have looked to for spiritual wisdom messes up, and it can leave people really shaken. I believe it often happens because leaders refuse to be vulnerable and real about their struggles. If they were to reach out for help and admit their weaknesses, they could have people pray with them and support them through it instead of it leading to disaster for themselves and those associated with them.

I recognise that I myself - in fact any of us - are in danger of doing the same if we are not careful. We are all frail, vulnerable, fallible humans with many faults, flaws, and blind spots. It's a wake-up call for me to make sure I'm living a life that is authentic. Although I'm not currently in a position of formal leadership, I profess to be a follower of Jesus. While I'll never be perfect, I need to do my best to aim to represent him well and to back up what I say I believe with how I live. I don't think people generally expect perfection, but they do want to see authenticity. I try to live in a way that is authentic, where I don't pretend everything is amazing when that's not the case. If I'm having a bad day, I try to share that rather than put on a false pretence. And when I'm struggling spiritually, I try to share honestly where I'm at with a trusted Christian friend.

I want to live life in a way that makes my Heavenly Father proud. So that my words, deeds, and thoughts please him, and back up my profession of being a Christ follower. I'll never get it totally right and I will fail every day, but I believe if we are honest about our shortcomings with some trusted people and we ask for forgiveness regularly and quickly, we can live an authentically imperfect life.

I think we also have to guard against enjoying the drama of other people failing. Maybe there's something in us that feels a bit better when we see someone else publicly fail. I have to admit I did feel quite smug watching Matt Hancock eat a sheep's bum in the bushtucker trial. Bottoms up Matt! It felt like the country was enjoying watching him being punished en masse. I think it's right to be angry and frustrated when people disappoint us, and I 100% think people should be held accountable for their actions. But I also believe we need to ensure we remember to take responsibility for ourselves - to look inside our own hearts and minds and evaluate if we are living in a way that is integral and that pleases our Father God. We will answer to him for our lives one day when we meet him face to face. This doesn't need to be a terrifying thought, but it can be a thought that spurs us on to do our very best with this short life we have been given.

So today is there anything that you are struggling with that, if allowed to grow in your life, could lead you down a path you don't want to tread? Do you see in yourself repeated behaviours and struggles that you can't seem to fight on your own? My husband and I have at times needed to sit down with trusted friends and tell them the battles we were facing in our marriage. It isn't easy to be so honest and vulnerable, in fact it can be extremely squirmy and awkward, but it might just save your life and relationships from imploding. I can honestly say that when I have chosen to bare my soul and my struggles with others it has only strengthened existing relationships and helped me to get through things feeling more loved and supported. It also means that the people you confide in feel they can share more honestly when things are tough for them too. And no one thus far has suggested I eat a sheep's bum as a form of punishment! Ph*ewe*!

YNWA - Sum up and Reflect:

Psalm 139 says that God knows when you sit and when you stand up. He knows the next word you will say before you say it. He knows your thoughts. Let knowing this spur you on to live authentically and to challenge any ungodly thoughts/behaviours/attitudes in your heart and life.

Spend some time praying for people you know who have recently failed publicly. Ask God to bring justice into the situation, and to help them and those who have been affected by it.

Above all, today, check your own heart. If you find anything that makes you feel like you've fallen short of God's standard (and that's all of us without exception), don't punish yourself by eating a sheep's bum! Confess it to God, find someone to be accountable to, accept God's unconditional love and grace and *move forward.*

Prayer:

God, today I bring to you my feelings of sadness, anger and disappointment towards people who have preached one thing and behaved in the opposite way. It's so saddening when it happens, and I bring before you everyone affected personally in the situations I'm thinking of right now. I pray for justice, grace and recompense for all involved. Please bring good out of what is a truly awful circumstance. I acknowledge today that I myself am only a few silly choices and compromises away from going down a path that's not good for me or for people who love me. Help me to adhere to your word for today to guard my heart. Help me to keep you first in my heart, and to live a life that is authentically imperfect, where I do my best to represent you well, but never give the appearance of having it all together when that's not the case. Thank you for accepting me with all of my faults and failings - help me to cling to you tighter for help to become more like you.

4th DECEMBER – 'CHAIRY' MARY

Luke 1:38 - "I am the Lord's servant, may it be to me as you have said."

Mary was an incredible woman. She was someone who naturally may well have been overlooked and underestimated by people around her. Just a young 'girl next door' type. One of the crowd, nothing special.

But not to God. God saw in her a godly, faith-filled, mature believer who he could trust with giving birth to Jesus - the saviour of the world. That is an incredible assignment to be entrusted with!

Sometimes in life we feel overlooked. We feel like people underestimate us, or they put us in a box linked to our job title or surname or class or age or race or gender. When this happens we can take encouragement from the Christmas story that God does not do this - he sees the treasure within us and he wants to pull it out and for us to live to our full potential. We need to be willing, like Mary was, to respond to his call. When the angel appeared to Mary and told her what God was asking of her, she responded by saying: "I am the Lord's servant, let it be to me as you have said" (Luke 1:38).

Mary was a young woman of character, who put her trust fully in God and whose heart was eager to respond to his call, despite the things people would say about her as a result of

God's strange mission for her. Can you even begin to imagine the gossip surrounding God's calling on Mary's life?

I've recently felt cheesed off a few times in various church gatherings I've been to, hearing comments from the front - and I quote: "women talk a lot more than men", "it's the man's job to put the bins out" (if I'd had any eggs on me I would have thrown them at the preacher at this point as that's literally my favourite household task - I live for bin day, no bins get missed on my watch I'll have you know) and "please could you help stack the chairs after the service - but it's a job for the men really."

The chair one really wound me up. It annoys me because it underestimates me and disqualifies me from participating for no good reason at all. I'm no Olympic athlete but I know I could stack chairs quicker than half the men in there. It also insults men who may not physically be able to stack the chairs. These general statements really get to me because they put people in boxes. Women are weak and chatty, men don't talk and are strong with super chair stacking powers. It's just ridiculous, and it's not my experience of the people I know!

Mary was far from a weak woman. She was brave, faith-filled, and mature in her walk with the Lord despite her young age. She was full of strength, dignity, and trust. If we're honest, what God asked her to do was beyond bonkers on a human level. It required a deep knowing of God and a trust in his plan that undoubtedly would have made Mary look crazy for being involved in. But she knew it was God's calling on her life, and she was eager and willing to step forward and be obedient. I reckon Mary could definitely out-stack some of the shepherds and wise men in the chair shifting department, and if it was bin day at the manger she could have handled that too - even after just giving birth!

The Christmas story really encourages me as it's full of 'normal' everyday people, who stepped up and stepped into God's role for them in the incredible miracle of Jesus' birth. They chose to disregard the view society had of them linked to their class or gender, and listened to what God said and how he wanted to use them in his plans. Joseph was spiritually in tune to know that Mary was telling the truth, and he supported her and became Jesus' adopted dad. The shepherds and kings were going about their business and responded in faith to the message of the angels and God-given dreams. So many supernatural experiences are involved in the Christmas story, involving ordinary people responding in faith to God's word.

YNWA - Sum up and Reflect:

Do you feel overlooked or invisible at the moment? Bring these thoughts and feelings before God now and let him speak into those frustrations.

People around you may not always see your value or your potential. They may have you in a box and underestimate or stereotype you. God does not do this. He knows you inside out and he has a unique role for you to play in his big picture story of salvation.

Ask him to reveal to you what this role is, and resist feeling 'less than,' as that's the opposite of how God sees you.

Be ready and willing, as Mary was, to respond when he calls you. And if there's any help needed with cleaning up after church, then stack those chairs like you just don't care! And watch out and holler in support for your church's 'Chairy Mary' showing all the blokes up!

Prayer:

God, there are times when I feel so disheartened because people overlook, underestimate or misunderstand me. Today, I choose to be encouraged by the characters in the Christmas story. Thank you for examples of ordinary people like Mary. Society would likely have undervalued her, yet you chose her to be a kingpin in your plan of salvation. Help me to process the feelings of disappointment in any areas of my life where I feel overlooked or invisible today. Encourage my heart that you have a special role that only I can fulfil, even in my ordinariness. Help me to develop the attitude that Mary had, that I am your servant and that I'm willing to step up and serve you in whichever way you see fit. Thank you that you know me inside out and you truly see and value me. Amen.

5th DECEMBER – THE JOHN LEWIS AD

John 1:14 - "The Word became flesh and pitched his tent among us."

I love the anticipation of watching the John Lewis Christmas ad each year. They are so creative with them, and they often carry a lovely message. (As well as trying to flog us their products!) There was the man on the moon (my fave so far), Edgar the dragon and Monty the penguin. So I was as eager as ever to view this year's offering.

When I did it really got to me. I cried as I watched it, and not in a 'happy tears' kind of way. It was actually really painful.

The advert shows a couple getting ready for Christmas, but it particularly focuses on the male partner, who is learning how to skateboard. It shows how he keeps trying to perfect the art of skateboarding and keeps failing. He makes progress though, and the advert ends with a knock at the door. A social worker stands on their doorstep with a nervous looking young girl next to her clutching a skateboard. The couple are obviously going to be foster carers for this girl, and the man has been desperately trying to master the art of skateboarding as a means of connecting with her. The advert ends by saying how John Lewis want to support the cause of children in care - a fantastic thing to do.

So why did it create such an emotional response from me?

Because my husband and I have just resigned as foster carers, and this has been a difficult thing for me to let go of.
Children being in loving families is the cause I feel most pas-
sionately about, as I feel it's so central to the rest of their lives.
I'm an adoptive mamma and have a passion to see children in
loving homes where they are valued, encouraged, and cele-
brated. We became foster carers two years ago, and for the first
year we were active in providing respite care each month. Then
for the last year *nothing* has happened. The organisation we
were fostering with have exhausted all respite options, and
while they could place us with a child full-time tomorrow, there
aren't any respite opportunities. I feel so gutted about this, as I
so wanted to make a difference in this area. I really believed
God was going to open a door of opportunity for us to support
a child through respite care. I had a real passion specifically to
foster a deaf child as I can sign. But for some reason God has
not opened this door, and I have to choose to continue to trust
him when I don't understand his ways. I have to believe that in
some way the last three years of the rigorous approval process,
the epic amount of training, the monthly supervisions, the un-
announced home visits and hours of assignments have not been
a waste of time (when in honesty it feels like a complete waste
of time from where I'm standing).

So this year as I watch the John Lewis advert I'm not filled
with Christmas cheer as I'd expected to be. It actually stings
quite a bit. It's a wonderful advert and a wonderful cause, but
for me personally it highlights what feels like the death of a
dream. It throws up questions about why God would allow us
to go through such a strenuous process and invest so much time
when it amounted to very little, and now we have had to actually end it. Gutted. I also feel like a failure, as we just didn't

have the capacity to do more. So many people I know have several kids (and also rear chickens in some cases!), plus they have jobs and social lives and they home school and make their own clothes and jam etc - and I'm left feeling a bit rubbish in comparison as I recognise that, in honesty, we couldn't cope with another child full-time as things stand. I wish I had greater capacity.

I'm not rushing to resolve this in my head. I often feel like we are encouraged to move on too quickly from pain and grief. I don't want to stay in this place forever, but for now I'm stopping here and embracing the fact that this is hard. That I don't understand what's happened, and that I feel very confused. That a big dream and desire of mine has not been fulfilled, and it means I may never care for any other children in our home. I'm being honest in my conversation with God that I'm wrestling to trust as I just don't understand. That I'm disappointed, sad, doubting if I heard him right in the first place, and wondering if we should ever have applied to become foster carers.

Sometimes life is really painful and we face many mysteries. What I am doing is continuing my dialogue with God. It's tempting to just think 'well forget it' and give up on talking to him. But I'm bringing my pain and confusion to him, and I'm asking for peace and for him to show me something of the 'why' of all of this - if he wants to. I'm also accepting that I may never know why, and I know I need to continue to trust him regardless of whether he gives me that insight or not.

YNWA - Sum up and Reflect:

When you feel sad, disillusioned, disappointed, confused and angry, God is right by your side walking with you through the pain. Look at the scripture we opened with today - Jesus was the word who became flesh and lived among us. Bring all of your hurt and pain to him in complete rawness and honesty. He is a God who truly understands our suffering, he wants you to share your innermost feelings with him.

Do your best to keep dialogue open with him and to trust and confess that he is good, even when your circumstances say the opposite is true.

Try to turn your reflection today to God who never wastes anything. You may feel similar to me, that things you've put your effort, energy and time into have been wasted. But maybe you and me will never know the impact of that energy, effort and time while we are here on earth. Ask God to bless and use all of the energy you have put into your personal endeavours and to help you trust that he will use it for his glory even if you never find out the specifics of how.

At Christmas particularly, we focus our attention on Jesus coming to earth in human form. Jesus chose to live among us and he experienced first-hand every range of emotion that we do. He truly understands the depths of grief and disappointment we feel. Bring it all to him, and know that he is walking with you through it and can genuinely empathise with you. The prophet Isaiah referred to Jesus as "a man of sorrows, familiar with suffering" (Isaiah 53:3). He *truly* understands our times of disappointment, sorrow and pain.

Prayer:

God, some things in life just don't make sense. I feel so passionate and sure of things and then when they don't work out in any way as I had hoped they would, it is so discouraging and confusing. I longed for you to use me in this way, and it's just not happened in the way I had envisioned it would. God, please will you meet me and minister to me in the middle of my pain, grief, and loss of this dream. Help me to continue talking to you and sharing my real and raw feelings. Thank you that you are always there to talk to, and that you want me to be honest about my struggles. I also thank you that you chose to become human and that you truly understand what it's like to face grief and disappointment. Help me to trust you each day as I process my disappointment, and I ask that in time you'll bring healing to these painful experiences. Amen.

6th DECEMBER – SILENT NIGHT

Matthew 6:34 - "Therefore do not worry about tomorrow, for tomorrow will worry about itself. Each day has enough trouble of its own."

Winter bugs are a flippin' nightmare. Our little girl doesn't fare too well during the Winter season as she picks up every bug that's doing the rounds. Having Down Syndrome means she has narrow tubes, so colds and coughs tend to be a bit worse, and can take her longer to shake off. She currently has a chest infection, and last weekend was like one long exhausting day as she literally didn't sleep for more than an hour at a time. She sounded like a mixture of Darth Vader and Frank Butcher (what a combo!) with her heavy chesty breathing and awful cough.

I really struggle during these sleepless situations. I often feel so overwhelmed, and I get very negative. I start to worry about all of the 'what ifs' - what if this goes on for another week, what if the meds don't clear it, what if I can't get to work, what if we never ever sleep again.

I spoke at a women's breakfast recently, and the lady running it wrote me a lovely card. On the front it said 'one day at a time.' During this snot-filled season I'm trying to really hold onto this advice.

"Yesterday is history, tomorrow is a mystery, today is a gift that's why we call it the present." That's a cheesy phrase I'd tend to roll my eyes at, but there is truth alongside the cheese here. Today *is* the gift that we have - snot or not!

Instead of being full of dread, worry, and stress about what ifs, I want to focus my energy on this day. It really is a gift, and I want to make the most of it: to love the people in front of me, to be grateful for all I have.

I'm trying to look for the little blessings even during these difficult, knackering, bug-filled, sleep-deprived days. The little gifts we can experience even when our days are not easy. I'm thankful for the gift of my parents who came to stay and looked after our girl for two days. I'm loved and supported and I'm grateful for that. I'm thankful for the gift of the doctor we saw who was so lovely with my girl. She kept saying "hello doctor" throughout our appointment - we had practised beforehand and she really delivered! Before we left he picked up her jacket and put it on for her. That was not his job but he showed care and kindness in that small act, and that was a real gift to me. I'm thankful for a hot cup of Yorkshire Tea (best teabag - no arguments!). I'm thankful for the gift of a friend who texts to see how we are doing and let us know she is praying for us. These little gifts are so precious. There are many little gifts within each day, and if we intentionally look for them we will spot them.

So we may not be having many silent nights at the moment, but I'm doing my best to take it 'one day at a time.' I'm deliberately looking for and showing gratitude for the little gifts within each day.

YNWA - Sum up and Reflect:

Life can be challenging and stressful in different ways for each one of us. Your current challenges will be different from mine, but we all experience times that make us feel stressed, tired, anxious, and despairing.

Every day is a gift and if we look carefully we will see many little gifts within each day - even on the very challenging days.

Don't waste time 'what if-ing.' Try to steer well clear of all of the negative 'what ifs' trying to sabotage your peace. Take it 'one day at a time' and actively look for the mini gifts in front of you. Make sure you show gratitude to God for all of the mini gifts you spot.

Make a list of every mini gift you have experienced today, and thank God for each of them.

Prayer:

Thank you God for this gift of life. It's certainly not always easy, and many different challenges come up. Help me not to become overwhelmed by all of the negative 'what ifs' surrounding my situation. Instead, help me to take it 'one day at a time' and to intentionally look for the many mini gifts that are to be found in each day. Thank you for your many mini blessings, even through dark and difficult days. Help me to actively look for them and to live with a grateful heart.

7ᵗʰ DECEMBER – CHRISTMAS BAKING

1 Corinthians 12:27 - "Now you are the body of Christ, and each of you is a member of it." (If you have time read 12:12-27.)

As I type this I've got a new brownie recipe in the oven. It's from the book *Eye Can Write* by Jonathan Bryan. If you're looking for a good book to read over the Christmas holidays, or for Christmas gift ideas, I can't recommend it highly enough.

Jonathan was born with cerebral palsy and has something called locked-in syndrome. He was unable to communicate his incredible intelligence until he was 9. A speech board was developed and he uses his eyes to spell out words. He wrote his book this way (when he was around the age of 12 I think) and it's an incredible read. His attitude is beyond exemplary - he describes his mission as being a voice to the voiceless. He campaigns for children with special needs to be taught how to read and write.

His faith in God is so personal and so strong. His outlook on life is so inspirational. In the face of incomprehensible struggles and challenges, he continually uses his life to love, serve, and advocate for others. He says this: "It doesn't matter how fragile, damaged, or broken our pot is, it can still be used to house the greatest treasure of all. Learning to be content with the jar you've been given and believing God made you for a purpose is the first part of your offering. I have to remember to daily rely on God's strength and not my own and to daily offer myself as a voice for the voiceless."*

At a time when we are still adjusting to life after Covid-19 and lockdowns, I'm looking at this extraordinary example of a young man who is 'locked-in' in ways most of us will never understand. Yet he continues to choose to give his life to helping others and reflecting his faith in Jesus.

Reading Jonathan's book has impacted me a lot and challenged me about not making assumptions about people's ability or what people may privately be facing that we are unaware of. It reminded me of the importance of really needing to take the time to truly get to know someone. I've seen lots of posts on social media along these lines recently, encouraging us to remember that we have very little idea what's *really* happening in another person's life. Let's take the time to listen, to understand, and to unlock the treasure in those around us. Especially those who are perhaps different from us who we may be guilty of overlooking due to our differences and perhaps a lack of understanding on our part.

Jesus modelled this so well, he often spent time with those who society disregarded or misunderstood. He chose to hang out with those who were very different to him, and he drew out the treasure within them. A great example that comes to mind is Zaccheus the tax collector. His business strategy was beyond dodgy, he ripped many people off and behaved in ways that were totally unacceptable. Yet an encounter with Jesus, who cheekily invites himself round to Zaccheus' house, leads to a total transformation. Zaccheus paid back four times what he owed the people he had swindled. This challenges me to try not to judge or overlook people, especially those not considered to be 'successful' or 'important' in our culture. Or those who are outright dodgy geezers like Zaccheus was.

Over the last five years I have been learning British Sign Language. I'm now competent enough to work with deaf people and I have a deaf friend who I love meeting up with for our 'Rise and Sign' bible studies. I'm so proud of the name of our group! I love that I have acquired this language, it's been crazy hard work as it's really not an easy thing to pick up, but it's *so* worth it. I now have relationships with some of the most amazing people, because we share a language and because I now understand a little of their culture and the many barriers they face in daily life.

It has blessed me to now call people friends who before I would never have been able to relate to. Engaging with the deaf community has widened and massively enriched my experience of life. It's truly wonderful. Things are improving for the deaf community, but they have been and continue to be so often overlooked and just not catered for in terms of access to things most of us take for granted. I'm not saying everyone should learn another language, but I am posing this question: 'What steps could you take to engage with people who are different to you, and who are perhaps misjudged or overlooked?'

That said, I think it's really important to make the point that people are not projects. We shouldn't jump in like smug little 'do-gooders' to 'save' other people. Our involvement needs to be out of a heart of love and mutuality, acknowledging that we have much to learn and receive from others along with any support we ourselves give.

YNWA - Sum up and Reflect:

We can use our unique body, personality, and circumstances to impact other people's lives for good. God designed us for community and wants us to help unlock the treasure in those around us. This means we must take time to listen, to be with, and to understand the people we come into contact with. Depth of relationship and truly knowing and being known only comes with love, time, patience, and intentionality.

We all have a unique part to play in 'the body of Christ.' Let's do our best to really know, value, and understand fellow members of that body, or those who do not yet belong to it.

Is there anyone in your life who you may have been underestimating, overlooking, or judging in any way? A person, or group of people who you recognise are overlooked, judged, or misunderstood in society? Anyone who you may come into contact with over the festive period? See if God highlights anyone to you today, and try in some way to deepen your understanding of them and look for ways to get to know the treasure within them this Christmas.

Perhaps in the next few days you could engage in some festive baking and reach out with an act of kindness to someone - ask God to show you who could be blessed by a brownie or gifted with gingerbread (shop bought is acceptable if you have a similar level of skill to me in the baking department - burn baby burn!).

Prayer:

God please will you help me to see others as you see them. I'm aware that I carry opinions and views of others that may not be accurate. Help me not to judge others based on what I can see or what I think I know about their culture or the challenges they face. Help me to be a person who actively looks for the treasure in others and who is willing to learn from people who are different to me. Thank you for the incredible example of Jonathan Bryan and the inspiration he is to the world. Help me to learn from him and look for ways to advocate for and support other people. Help me to be gracious, patient, and kind, especially over the next couple of weeks as I spend time with family or friends who I may not fully click with or understand. Give me the desire to take the time to see things from their perspective and to deal with them with kindness and with the aim to pull out the treasure in them. Amen.

Recommended reading: *Eye Can Write* by Jonathan Bryan. His delicious brownie recipe is in the book :)

* https://www.youtube.com/watch?v=cPh8wUg9Auw – Jonathan Bryan – Thy Kingdom Come

8th DECEMBER – SECRET SANTA

Romans 12: 6-8 - "We have different gifts according to the grace given to us."

I chuckled to myself when I overheard a conversation at work this morning. Someone said: "I'm not being miserable but I've decided to remove myself from our team's secret Santa. I'm sick of getting rubbish gifts every year, I'm bored of toiletry sets, and chocolates are just a cop out." I have to admit that although I love the secret Santa game, I think my colleague makes a fair point. Secret Santa situations can often become an opportunity to recycle gifts, where we inflict our unwanted gifts on others, knowing that we remain unidentified as the giver of tatt!

Fortunately, when God gives us gifts and talents it's entirely different to the way most of us approach the secret Santa game. God does not recycle gifts and talents - he doesn't give us someone else's cast off gifts. It's not a slap-dash, grab something from the unwanted gift drawer situation. God designs each person with great thought and detail as a bespoke and valuable individual. God is a wonderful creator and every person on this planet is a unique creation possessing different gifts and talents.

I remember catching a friend out on the recycling gifts front one year, though I've never told her! She gave me a gift and hadn't realised that on the box there was a 'to and from' section which another friend of ours had filled in with her name on! The gift was not meant for me, it did not have my name on it. (But it was chocolate, so I gladly scoffed the lot!)

The gifts that God graciously gives us *do* have our names written all over them. There is real intent, planning, and thought in God's gift list. He delights in gifting us with different skills and abilities that we can use to help others and to bring glory to him. I have often wished that God had given me different gifts if I'm honest. I've longed to be more intelligent, more practical, and more outgoing. I am a half introvert, half extrovert (which apparently is an 'ambivert'), but I have an increasing leaning towards being an introvert. I just love time on my own in coffee shops, writing and studying. I also enjoy meeting friends and family and spending time with people I love, or meeting new people, but I need a decent chunk of time on my own to restore my energy. I quite like public speaking and preaching when I've had time to prepare what I'm going to say, but if you put me on the spot I'm no good at all, my brain doesn't work quickly! Both myself and my husband are more listeners than talkers. It's the way God has wired us and that's perfectly fine. We may not be as exciting to be around as people who can tell a good joke or an interesting story, but listening is an important and often overlooked gift that can really help others to feel heard and understood.

Throughout my life I've often wished I could be more like this person or that person and have this gift or that gift. But more recently, as I approach my 40's, I'm seeing the way God has made me and the gifts he's given me differently. Instead of resisting it and wishing I was more of a 'life and soul of the party' girl, I'm embracing the fact that God has made me more of a quiet and reflective person (and I'm unapologetic that I like being in my pj's by 5pm and in bed by 9pm!). Being more reflective means that I enjoy writing, and I hope that the things I write, like this devotional, will be used by God to help others. God wasn't short of an extrovert gift in his drawer so therefore I missed out: I'm created exactly the way he intended me to be. So if you come across me in a coffee shop feel free to buy me a one-shot latte then jog on so I can enjoy my time alone! (I might give you five minutes of chit chat time if you buy me a caramel shortbread to go with the coffee!)

As you give out your (hopefully not recycled - but we've all done it!) gifts this Christmas, remember that God has given you gifts, skills, and talents, and this has been an intentional decision by your Heavenly Father. Embrace and celebrate the unique creation that you are and be determined to use every gift and skill to glorify God and bless others. Don't see any of your gifts as insignificant. Often the people with the more razzle dazzle gifts do get seen and get more attention, it's just the way it works sometimes. But I want to encourage you to be determined to be your authentic self, designed by God with an incredible ability to have a significant impact in this world. Build on the skills and gifts God has given you, and thank him for them and for your unique personality and contribution to the world.

YNWA - Sum up and Reflect:

You have been uniquely designed by your Heavenly Father. He has given you good gifts and talents that he wants you to embrace, enjoy, and engage in to bless others and bring glory to his name. You are a wonderful creation. There is nothing recycled or half-hearted about God's approach to designing you. Embrace who he has made you to be, thank him for it and use your unique personality to reach out to others.

Make a list of the gifts you believe God has given to you. Are you using them? In what ways could you develop them and use them even more effectively?

Think of someone you know and encourage them today - send them a message listing the good gifts and qualities you see in them.

Prayer:

God I thank you that you give each one of us a bespoke gift package. You do not recycle gifts! You have intentionally designed and created us with love and forethought and have equipped us to make a unique mark on this planet for you. Help me as I reflect on my own strengths and gifts today. If there are any I'm unaware of, bring them to my attention. If there are any that I'm ignoring or are underused, please nudge me to start to develop and use them for your glory. Please bring to my mind someone who needs to be encouraged today, and as I message them to tell them the good gifts I see in them, let them be boosted and blessed and give them a renewed determination to use their own unique skill set for you. Amen.

9ᵗʰ DECEMBER - NATIVITY

Zephaniah 3:17 – "The Lord your God is with you, the Mighty Warrior who saves. He will take great delight in you; in his love he will no longer rebuke you, but will rejoice over you with singing."

This morning I went to watch my daughter in her school nativity. It was such a wonderful, heartwarming experience. It didn't start off brilliantly as we had to queue outside in the freezing cold, and it's such a frosty day today. I couldn't feel my toes, but there was no way I was losing my place near to the front of the queue, so I stayed put, hands stuffed in my pockets, shuffling my numb trotters around in my boots. I was outraged that a total of three parents thought it was acceptable to queue jump nearer to their pals at the front. I did lots of eye-rolling and huffing to passively aggressively show my disapproval. At least my rising blood pressure helped my temperature to go up a bit.

Anyway, we finally got inside and I bagged a seat on the front row. It was well worth the frozen toes to bag a spot right at the front. I was about two metres away from my daughter and I was so pleased to have such a close-up view of her performing. Her class were singing and signing to Christmas songs throughout the nativity play. My girl sang, smiled, laughed, and looked like she was having an absolute ball. It was a delight to watch her in action, and for her to keep catching my eye with her cheeky grin - so chuffed with herself. I felt quite emotional as I walked home, just bursting with pride in her. I was so captivated with her that I hardly looked at anyone else in the room, my eyes were fixed on the most gorgeous girl my eyes have ever seen.

It reminded me of how God feels when he looks at us. His heart swells with pride. We are his children, his creation. But unlike me, God has the incredible ability to focus on us all at the same time - that's utterly mind blowing! Omnipresence dot com! Just stop for a minute and reflect on the fact that God is always aware of you, you are always on his mind, his gaze is always on you. This motivates me to want to live in a way that makes him proud. Not in a pressured way where I feel terrified of putting a foot wrong. My daughter didn't do a 'perfect' performance by any stretch, but that in no way detracted from my overwhelming pride and love for her. I believe it's the same with God. He hears the duff notes in our 'performance,' he sees when we are getting a bit tired and wish the song would finish, or when we pick our nose or scratch our bum (!) when we forget his eyes are on us or we're just generally fed up. But as I watched my daughter I could see her confidence and security in my love for her. She could see my eyes were on her, that I was attentive to her and that I love her deeply - it was written all over her face. She knows that I'm delighted with her, she is secure in her identity as a much-loved child. I want to develop this kind of relationship with God. That I know that he is for me, that I'm his beloved child, that even when I nose pick and bum scratch and fail in so many ways, he doesn't kick me off the cast list. I want to look at him with the same confidence I saw in my daughter's face as she looked at me today. To live assured that I know I am loved, I know I am accepted, I know I am the apple of his eye. I want to be able to give him a cheeky

smile and have a twinkle in my eye as I go about my life knowing that I'm eternally loved and accepted, and that I'm the star
of the show to him.

On the show *Strictly Come Dancing* Bruce Forsyth used to
say "You're my favourite" - it became one of his catchphrases
that he said to every contestant. I can't believe I'm going to
compare God to Bruce Forsyth, but here we are - I think God
can honestly say that same catchphrase to each of us - 'you're
my favourite.' When we are born again, each one of us becomes
his much-loved child and his loving eyes are always on us. The
bible says that he sings over us and takes great delight in us.
(Zephaniah 3:17.)

I also think it's important that we live for his applause only.
Yes, encouragement from others is a bonus: it's nice when that
happens and we *should* encourage and build one another up.
But above all, it's his opinion of us that should make us want
to give our all in loving and serving him, and making the performance of our life count - all for his glory.

YNWA - Sum up and Reflect:

Do you struggle to live knowing that you are eternally loved
and accepted by God, regardless of how well you think you are
'performing'?

Be determined to develop an awareness and appreciation of
how much you are loved by your Heavenly Father. He is atten-
tively watching the 'performance' of your life and is longing to
see you reach your potential and cheering for you louder than
anyone else. Make a decision to give this life your all and to
live to make him proud.

If you are watching a relative in a nativity this year, think about the emotions you feel as you watch, and reflect on how much more God loves and rejoices over us than we do over our loved ones.

Adopt my daughter's confident little attitude, and be encouraged that when you are born again into the family of God, you are *eternally* loved, accepted and championed.

Prayer:

Thank you God that you are a loving Heavenly Father. Thank you that you are always interested in and attentive to what is happening in my life. But even more than that, thank you that you take delight in me, that I am your beloved child and you rejoice with singing over me. Help me to do my best to live for your applause only, and to live with a confidence that I am always loved, cherished and accepted by you. You are a good Father and I'm so grateful for your unending love, mercy and goodness to me. Amen.

P.S. if you could sort out those parents who pushed in that'd be great.

10th DECEMBER – DECK (HALF OF) THE HALLS

1 Corinthians 13:4-7 - "Love is patient, love is kind. It does not envy, it does not boast, it is not proud. It does not dishonour others, it is not self-seeking, it is not easily angered, it keeps no record of wrongs. Love does not delight in evil but rejoices with the truth. It always protects, always trusts, always hopes, always perseveres."

I heard on the radio that last weekend was 'treekend,' where people who have fake Christmas trees get them up and twinkling! It's taken us a few more days to get sorted, but the tree is finally done... well half of it is. Our tree doesn't really fit in our lounge. It did in our last house, but isn't quite the right fit for this house. However, I'm too Scroogey to shell out for another tree, so this one is staying! The only place it just about fits is in the corner of the room by the dining table. Only half of it is in view with it being backed into a corner, therefore only half of it gets decked! I have some friends who are disgusted by this and think it should be beautifully adorned the whole way round! I disagree - my tree, my choice. A half-decked tree is good for me!

My half-decked tree reminds me of a theory of mine: that only nicely presenting the bit of tree that people see can be reflected in our internal lives. We all like to portray a certain image to others (and I'm not necessarily only talking about our physical image, although we often do like it to appear that our baubles are in the correct place if you will!). We want our personality to twinkle as perfectly as the lights on our trees (well, on half of mine) do. We present a version of ourselves that is put together, all in order, no damage or bare branches, no bulbs out.

I've heard it said that 'who you are at home is who you really are.' Meaning that when we are in the comfort of our own home not trying to perform or impress others, we are the real deal. I find this challenging as I recognise how I don't fare too well in regards to the real 'at home' me! Sometimes the way I speak or respond to my husband and my daughter is much less kind and twinkly than if I was at work or out with friends. There's a degree to which we should absolutely be able to relax, be ourselves, and not feel pressure to impress when we are in our own homes. I'm a lover of pjs and loungewear and quiet times chilling together without the pressure of having to try and engage in interesting conversation. We need time to relax, recover, and recharge at home. But this is not an excuse for a constant 'half-tree' approach to our nearest and dearest.

I often snap at my husband and can be very sarcastic in a way I would never be with colleagues and (heaven forbid) with people at church. But my husband and my daughter are two of the most important people to me. I don't want them to constantly get the 'naked tree' side of me. There will be times that are really tough when the 'naked tree' me will be present. That's part of life, and we have to show grace to each other in these times. Our naked tree sides should absolutely be loved, helped, and embraced as it's part of the human experience for all of us. No one permanently twinkles. But 'naked tree me' should not be a *permanent* fixture in our relationships with our close family. I'm very challenged by this as at home I'm very inclined to be snappy and sarcastic, and I know I need to work on this and make sure my close ones get some twinkle time. They are the most significant people in my life and I recognise that they should get the best of me, not the dregs.

YNWA - Sum up and Reflect:

Make sure that those closest to you, who God has graciously blessed you with, don't get the naked tree version of you *all of the time*. We all have hard times and times when we fail and are not twinkling on all cylinders, but we need to ensure the people we live with don't constantly cop the naked tree version of us.

We need to ensure we have quality time with our close family, along with kind hearts and kind words on our lips. I can so often be guilty of giving my best at work or with friends and then I don't have much left to give at home.

Do a little twinkle assessment and see if you need to turn up the twinkle with your nearest and dearest. Maybe that means cutting back on some other activities to give you back your capacity for twinkle time at home.

Look at the scripture for today from 1 Corinthians 13 and think of each of the characteristics of love as a twinkly light on a Christmas tree. Do a little twinkle assessment and see if any of your bulbs may need adjusting or replacing. I'm certainly challenged that many of mine do. Don't overwhelm yourself - try to work on one thing for starters during this festive season. I'll be kicking off with some work on my patience bulb. Lord have mercy and help me on that front!

Prayer:

God, as we head into the Christmas season and I have more time with friends and family, I pray you will help me to give my best to my nearest and dearest. Life is so busy and demanding and it can be easy to come home and have nothing left to give, or to be running on empty. I need time to relax and unwind at home, but prompt me to give some twinkle time to those I live with. Challenge me if there's anything in my life that needs to go or to be stripped back to give me more time and capacity to love my family better. Thank you for my loved ones who you have graciously given to me, and help me to value and appreciate them. Please highlight one of the facets of love from the Corinthians passage for me to focus on improving on through this festive season. Amen.

11ᵗʰ DECEMBER – CHRISTMAS JUMPERS

John 10:10 - "The enemy comes to steal, kill and destroy, I have come that they may have life and have it to the full."

I love a Christmas jumper. I usually go full on sparkly and colourful with 3D elements, but this year I opted for a much more understated Christmas jumper. I'm currently working in a sixth form college as a communication support worker. This role involves me going to lectures with students who are deaf and signing the lessons in British Sign Language to them. So when I saw a company called Deaf Identity were producing their own Christmas jumpers I really wanted to support their business and buy one. I ordered a black jumper with gold writing on it that said 'Mistletoe and Sign.' I thought this was a hilarious Christmas pun and couldn't wait to show it off to the deaf students at college. It turns out that 16-19 year olds do not know the song *Mistletoe and Wine* or even who Cliff Richard is, so it was quite a tumbleweed moment. Not exactly the hilarious giggles I had imagined!

I've been learning sign language for five years now, and I've recently completed the final level of it. I started to learn sign language when I met a deaf lady at church and realised what an isolating world it can be for deaf people - thumbs up and smiles are a good start, but can only get you so far in communication. I love that now we can meet up and giggle and she regularly signs 'naughty' to me when I'm being cheeky - we know each other well now because we can speak the same language. This level of relationship would not have been possible without sharing a language. I love sign language, it's such an interesting, fun, and beautiful way of communicating.

Myself and a friend at church decided to sign the carol service for our deaf friend who is always keen to attend when signing is provided. Even though I sign for my job, I was more nervous about doing it than I had expected to be. One reason for this is the Christmas lingo - I don't know about you but I don't say 'hark' or 'Gloria in excelsis deo' on a daily basis, so knowing how to translate and then sign these things isn't always easy! Thank the Lord for Google to tell me what these terms mean in English as a starting point!

When I woke up on the morning of the carol service my mind was bombarded by a list of reasons why I shouldn't be doing it including:

You don't know enough Christmas vocabulary.

You'll have a mind blank and won't know what to sign.

You aren't good enough.

You look tired and haggard and shouldn't be stood at the front.

Imposter syndrome was well and truly trying to take a hold.

Fortunately on this occasion I was able to shake this off and crack on and do it anyway. One thing that's really helped me is the writing of a guy called Jon Acuff who talks about changing the 'soundtracks' in your head. So I did my best to flip the thoughts and soundtracks in my head around as follows:

I may not yet be fluent in this amazing language, but I can communicate a good chunk of it.

Only two people in the room will actually know if it makes
no sense.

I am doing my best to communicate so my deaf friend can
enjoy a Christmas service, it doesn't have to be perfect.

No one gives a rat's ass how tired I do or don't look, I just
need to get over it and get on with it.

I really don't want to be held back in life by negative
thoughts and voices. I know where they come from ultimately
- the enemy wants me to be incapacitated, to do nothing and to
make no attempt to help anyone or do any good. I'm just not
accepting this. So I may not be perfect at signing, and I may
well look tired and old, but I will not be held back by these
things - I'm going forward and I'm going to try my best to make
a difference on this planet. I'd encourage you to do the same.
Try your hardest to reframe the negative thoughts that flood
your mind, and no matter how true they appear, crack on and
don't be held captive by them. You have a lot to offer and we
have to step out and take risks to get better at things, so just go
for it. Even if you have to do your thing wearing a hilarious
Christmas jumper that no one else understands.

YNWA - Sum up and Reflect:

God cheers you on every step of your journey. However,
you have an enemy that wants to rob you of your courage, gifting, and ultimately your effectiveness for God. However real
the thoughts he plants in your mind seem, try to change the
soundtrack and just go for it. Step out, take risks, take opportunities to grow and develop. Refuse to let fear and insecurity

stop you from stepping into the future God has for you. God is for you!

What are the negative soundtracks that replay in your mind? Make a list of them.

For each negative one, come up with one that counteracts it with God's truth, and do your best to play that soundtrack rather than the negative one. Write the new ones on post its and stick them around your house to help to remind and reinforce to you the positive thoughts that you want to live by.

Prayer:

I really want to make a difference for you God. Often, when I step out and take a risk in wanting to make a difference, there's a backlash of negativity. I feel insecure, unqualified, and at times overwhelmed by the negativity in my mind. I want to be involved in bringing hope and life to this world. Help me to quickly spot the negative soundtracks and to weigh them up against what you say about me. Help me not to be gripped by fear and negativity, but to move forward in faith and confidence in you. Amen.

Recommended reading: *Soundtracks* by Jon Acuff

12ᵗʰ DECEMBER – THE DASH

1 Thessalonians 5:16-18 - "Rejoice always, pray continually, give thanks in all circumstances; for this is God's will for you in Christ Jesus."

Today's thought is a pretty sombre one, but it's one that I pray brings real hope and a determination to really live life to the full. From the title, you might think the reference is to a 'Santa dash,' or the line from *Jingle Bells* about 'dashing through the snow,' or a nod to the reindeer called Dasher. But it doesn't relate to any of these festive offerings. I'll explain the reference to 'the dash' later on.

First of all, I want to tell you about a wee Scotsman called Robert, who our lives collided with around 8 years ago. My husband Rod has always travelled a lot for work, and in the days before we had our daughter Chloe (we refer to these times as BC), I was sometimes able to go along with him. This particular work trip was to Scotland. I had spent a year at bible college in Scotland when I was 18, and so was happy to go back as I was a fan of the place, especially as I had grown to really love the music of The Proclaimers during my time there. Their song *Let's Get Married* was included in our wedding service. I didn't get away with walking down the aisle to *500 Miles* unfortunately.

The church Rod was going to said that a couple from there would host us, which was very kind of them. It's always a little nerve wracking staying with people you don't know, however within the first 30 seconds I knew I needn't have worried - in fact I recognised that I'd potentially met my match in terms of sass and cheeky/dry humour. We pulled up on the drive and a wee bald Scotsman came out to meet us. Rod grabbed his huge metal magic trick case out of the car and plonked it down on the gravel driveway. Robert looked me straight in the eye and in his broad Scottish accent said "So this is your makeup case is it?" Ooosh. I liked him instantly - I knew I would be able to be cheeky and not have to be polite all weekend! Robert and his wife Libby were so easy to get on with, we really clicked with them and enjoyed getting to know them over the weekend we spent in their home. Robert introduced us to 'dirty chips' and he was evangelical about his electric potato masher! He could've flogged loads of them on QVC. He was so passionate about his wee tatty masher!

One of the days we were there, we had agreed to leave at a certain time to get to the venue where Rod was speaking. Rod was pacing around their lounge 25 minutes before said agreed departure time. I caught Robert's eye and he raised an eyebrow at me and shook his head discreetly. I knew we were kindred spirits, both cheesed off by the premature pointless pacing! It was a really good and fruitful weekend. I spoke at a women's event and got to hear some of the reviews of my talk while I had an apres-preach wee - unbeknownst to them! I was randomly compared to 'that comedian who plays Doc Martin's secretary' which was a new one on me!

Several years later, we made another trip to Scotland and were able to introduce Robert and Libby to our lovely daughter. It was so good to catch up with them, and Robert, a keen photographer, took some amazing snaps of Chloe in a Scottish 'Jimmy hat.'

Around a year or so ago, Robert was sadly diagnosed with terminal cancer. He wrote a series of blogs about his health challenge, which I enjoyed following. He had such a real, honest, yet positive and faith-filled perspective on what he was experiencing. He encouraged readers to live life to the full, to choose to see the good, to be determined to stay thankful even through immense difficulty and pain, and to make the most of every day and every moment. Robert died just a few months ago.

The Dash was a poem that was read at Robert's funeral. To read it in full you can find it online. To give you a flavour of the poem, I'm going to quote in full the author, Linda Elliot's updated version, called *The Dash Between*:

There are two important dates
around the life that we live
that reflect the time we're given
to laugh, to love, to live.

And between the date when we arrive
and the date we go away,
there exists a horizontal line
that captures every single day.

Because these days we're living
seem to vanish in a flash,
we need to make the most of
that special little dash.

We are blessed with opportunities
as we tread the grounds of earth

to build the loving legacy
our own dash will be worth.

To focus on what matters,
not on possessions owned or bought,
and smile every chance we get,
and to live with all we've got.

To appreciate the here and now
as each moment will unfold
because we're never told beforehand
how much time our dash will hold.

So, if you need to make some changes,
let this be the day you start
to make a difference with your life,
show the love that's in your heart.

For how you spend this life
will someday be defined
by everything that is remembered
In the dash you leave behind.

Robert: thank you for modelling how to walk through such a challenging and painful time with honesty, integrity, humour, and faith. Whenever my husband is pacing pointlessly, or we are eating dirty chips, or I hear the sound of an electric potato masher, I will smile and give thanks for your life and for the impact your faith through a really difficult time had on me. See you up there one day - get The Proclaimers on, and have some dirty chips and a Jimmy hat ready for me please.

YNWA - Sum up and Reflect:

Spend some time today reflecting on how you are spending your dash, whatever the circumstances of your dash may currently be.

Take note of the wisdom gleaned from Robert's life, and how through an incredibly challenging time he was able to hold on to faith, hope, humour, and love.

Thank God for someone you know who is walking through a challenge with real grace. Ask God to help them through whatever it is they are facing.

Whenever you hear a festive 'dash' related reference in the next couple of weeks, try to stop briefly and reflect on the brevity of life, as well as the opportunities your life holds for doing good.

Whatever is happening in our dash, let's be determined, as Robert was, to look for the good, to be positive, faith-filled, and thankful.

Prayer:

God, I thank you for the life you have given to me. I'm aware that I can so often waste time worrying or fixating on things that just don't matter. Give me a sense of perspective today, remind me that this life is short and help me to focus on all of the good and to be determined to do as much good as I can during my short dash here on earth. Thank you for the example of Robert who held on tight to you through a really difficult circumstance. Help me to learn from him and his incredible attitude. I bring my 'dash' before you now, please reignite me today and help me to live and serve you well within it. Amen.

https://lindaellis.life/ - The Dash Between

13ᵗʰ DECEMBER – CARROTS AND COMPROMISE

Philippians 2:3-4 - "Do nothing out of selfish ambition or vain conceit. Rather, in humility value others above yourselves, not looking to your own interests, but each of you to the interests of others."

Today I'm thinking about two different Kevins. One is the happy, helpful, heroic, heartwarming, and humorous little Kevin the Carrot off the Aldi Christmas adverts. The other is the stroppy, sarcastic, snarly, snidey, self-obsessed Kevin the Teenager played by Harry Enfield. During the festive season especially, I feel like I often swing at times more to the Kevin the Teenager end of the Kevin spectrum.

Things have changed a lot for our family since the days of Covid-19 and lockdowns. I have started on a new career path, going out to work four days a week, but my husband still works from home a lot. It's a very different scenario to how it used to be when he always went out to work.

We have needed to learn more than ever the art of compromise in our relationship. I remember through the lockdowns I was told to 'turn that music down' and to 'get off the internet' as it was interfering with my husband's video calls. An old colleague even cheekily messaged me to tell me to get off my own internet as their meeting kept freezing. How rude. My reply was not the most polite! Kevin the Teenager mode in full swing - "this is so unfair."

How is it fair to be told to get off my own internet and to shut down Celine Dion when she's going full pelt on her greatest hits (and I may be belting them out too)?! What is life coming to? So unfair!!

However, maybe I should 'think twice' about my stroppy Kevin the Teenager attitude?! I'd like to be forgiving 'but it's all coming back to me now!'

I also remember that during lockdown my college course in British Sign Language had to switch to being entirely on Zoom. It was a three-hour class and it was *full on*. The first few times the screen kept freezing, and it was then that I understood the frustration of trying to focus and keep up in online meetings when others in the house are hogging the internet.

Seeing things from someone else's point of view helps us to be more reasonable in our response to their requests. We are then more inclined to slap our inner Kevin the Teenager in the face with a wet fish and to choose to respond in a Kevin the Carrot helpful, positive, and accommodating way.

Compromise is so important in these post-lockdown days when we are adjusting to new ways of living and working. Compromise means us working together and making concessions to help each other out, and to help make something work for the overall good. Give and take. All relationships and households need compromise on all sides in order to really thrive.

The bible goes even further than this though (sometimes the bible gets on my nerves as it's so often the polar opposite of what I naturally want to do). It says "do nothing out of selfish ambition or vain conceit, but in humility, value others above yourself." (Philippians 2:3.)

That's a huge challenge to us all as we spend more time cooped up together during the cold weather, darker days, and upcoming festivities. But this kind of attitude and spirit really helps to build a happy life and home. If all of us were to consider others as more important than ourselves, our homes would be transformed. I'll try and remember that the next time I want to belt out *My Heart Will Go On* along with Celine and my husband is on a video call. Maybe.

YNWA - Sum up and Reflect:

Living and working closely with others can be challenging. Trying to approach situations of conflict with kindness and Kevin the Carrot like consideration is much better than responding stroppily like Kevin the Teenager. If you are struggling with a disagreement or area of compromise, try to view it from the other person's perspective.

Carrots allegedly help you to see in the dark, but God's word and the Holy Spirit most definitely shed light on the areas of our lives that are dark and bleak and need some attention. Ask God to show you any area of your life where you need to compromise - and even beyond that, where you need to consider another person's interests *above your own.*

Prayer:

God, help me to be a person who gets better at the art of compromise. Help me to look out for the needs of all of those around me, and to do my best to make sacrifices and compromises in order for them to thrive and succeed. Holy Spirit, I ask you to shed light on the areas of my life where I have become self-focused and nudge me on relationships where I have not considered the needs of others as I recognise I should. Help me during this Christmas season to regularly stop and consider if I'm thinking of others and to actively look for ways to support those around me more effectively. Help me to quickly recognise if I'm flipping into Kevin the Teenager mode and help me to flip back quickly to carrot o'clock when this happens! Amen.

14Th DECEMBER – CAN APPLE CRUMBLE KEEP YOU HUMBLE?

Psalm 94:18 - "When I said, "My foot is slipping," your unfailing love, Lord, supported me."

I've never been a fan of the traditional Christmas pudding. It's not that I think it's horrendous, it's just that I feel there are many more worthy puddings to be scoffed on Christmas Day. My top three all-time puddings, since you asked, would have to be sticky toffee pudding, banoffee pie, and apple crumble. We've decided on a crumble for this year's Christmas Day desert, so it's all good in the pud!

A couple of months back we were given some apples from a friend's garden. I'd not made a crumble for years so thought I'd have a go - 'you can't go wrong as crumbles are easy' I thought. You can probably guess how this story is going to end.

I found a nice recipe by Nigel Slater for a crunchy, oat-topped crumble. *Lush*. Come on then Nigey baby, let's get ready to crumble.

I wasn't sure whether to peel the apples. In the recipe good old Nige didn't say so, and I thought to myself, well it doesn't matter as the skins will just add fibre anyway.

Let's just say it was not a very appealing (a-peeling) crumble! The apple skin slid off and we had to fish it out as we went along. Most days since 'crumblegate' my husband enjoys reminding me of this failure. He shakes his head in despair that I didn't peel them. He's considering writing a second book called *The Peel Deal*. This is a highly amusing joke as he wrote a book called *The Real Deal* - try and stop laughing so much and read on.

Last weekend another friend kindly gave us some apples and I decided to redeem myself in the crumble stakes. The one that I baked yesterday was much better, it was so good I'm insisting everyone now refers to me as 'Bezza' as I feel like I'm now a younger version of the esteemed Mary Berry. I enjoyed scoffing a big portion drenched in custard while I dreamt of receiving a Hollywood handshake for my services to crumbledon!

When it comes to mistakes in life they can vary in intensity. The one I've shared is no big deal really (though my husband would argue otherwise). Other mistakes have different consequences and can leave us feeling down, ashamed, and like we are a permanent failure. One thing that blows my mind about God is how kind, gracious, and forgiving he is. No matter how many mistakes we make and how many times we fail, he still loves us. Once we tell him our mistakes and ask him to forgive us he does so straight away and never ever holds it against us. The bible says he remembers our sins no more. (Hebrews 8:12.)

The bible is full of people who did amazing things for God, many of them we think of as heroes of the Christian faith. But the reality is that they messed up in many different ways. Noah got drunk. Moses killed someone. Abraham lied. Thomas doubted. David slept with another man's wife. Perhaps one of the most random - Jacob covered his arms in goat skin to convince his dad that he was his brother and so deceived his father. The bible doesn't hide the failures of these characters. If you have sinned, failed, or messed up, you are in good company. Have a heart to heart with God and confess anything to him that's weighing you down, any area of weakness or failure. He will forgive you and remove the burden of your sin from your shoulders. Maintain an attitude of humility in the way that you approach the failures and mistakes of others. We all fall short and most of us do so regularly. We receive such deep mercy and grace from God, and we must do our best to extend that to those who fail us or who share their failures with us.

So my festive reflection for today (as I dream about my apple crumble pud on Christmas Day) is: 'Our failures and mistakes can help us stay humble, but they don't need to make us crumble.' You are so very welcome! In relation to your failures and mistakes, be humble but don't crumble.

YNWA - Sum up and Reflect:

Jesus was born to save us from all our sin and failure. If you have things that are weighing you down, give them to him today. Say sorry and move forward confidently, knowing that you are loved and free.

Don't let past failures leave you stunted in your growth as a Christian. Let them keep you humble and grateful for Jesus, who came to this planet to help. We all fail and make mistakes. Walk humbly (not crumbly) before God and others.

Bring the ways in which you feel you've failed God this week before him now. Be reminded that his great love for you never fails, and when you stumble, you don't have to crumble.

Reflect on the scripture for today: that when your foot slips and you begin to stumble, God's unfailing love will support you.

Next time someone you know messes up, try to approach the situation with humility, recognising that you yourself have needed forgiveness, grace, and support.

Prayer:

Thank you for this amazing scripture from the Psalms, that when I feel I'm slipping or I'm about to stumble, you are there and willing to support me. Your love for me never fails regardless of how many times I stumble. Thank you that because of your great love and forgiveness, when we do stumble we don't have to crumble. You pick us up, dust us off, and give us the strength to try again. Help me to reflect this in some way to others who share their faults and failures with me. Amen.

15Th DECEMBER – FROM SEED TO SEQUOIA

1 Corinthians 12:26 - "If one part suffers, every part suffers with it; if one part is honoured, every part rejoices with it."

This week I heard a song on a Christmas playlist called *Seasons* by Hillsong. It's a good few years old now, but it was new to me. It's really helped me where I'm currently at, and I hope the following thoughts help if you are in a similar place.

The song is all about how God plants seeds of promises and dreams within us but there is often a long wait involved, and various seasons to go through, before we see the seed grow and the promise fulfilled. Seasons talks about a promise going from 'seed to sequoia.' I had to Google it as I had no idea what the chuff a sequoia was. A sequoia, I now know, is a dock-off tree that can live for more than 3,000 years. Type it in Google images, they are impressive! It's insane that one of those massive trees started off as a tiny seed. Apparently the seed actually needs some of the harsh conditions of Winter for it to eventually flourish and grow into a dock-off sequoia.

I think most of us struggle with waiting, endurance, and patience during the harsh 'Winter' seasons. I've mentioned previously that my Christmas tree is artificial - and there's nowt wrong with that in my opinion! I do love real trees, but I want a Christmas tree that I can get up quickly with minimum mess and fuss. I don't want to get my tinsel in a tangle.

However, when it comes to seeds of promises and dreams from God, there isn't a quick fix, artificial sequoia option. We have to think long haul, and we will have many lessons to learn in preparation along the way. We have to be determined to dig deep and keep believing, and keep moving forward in hope and expectation, even in the face of strong adversity and the bleak conditions of Winter.

The bridge of the song talks of the need to look to the future and see the promise, to wait well as God continues to work. It also highlights how God could have saved humanity in a click of his fingers, yet he chose to send Jesus as a human. God doesn't rush to fulfil promises, he takes his time (which is literally never in agreement with my timetable!).

God's plan to save us could have been a quick puff of smoke, job done. Yet, as the song reminds us, he chose to send Jesus as a child. Nine months growing in Mary's womb. Growing from baby to toddler to teen to man. Not a quick process. This is so often the case with God's plans. Which irritates the life out of me frequently, if I'm honest. I'd often just prefer him to say the word and jobs a good'un, so to speak.

But there must be a reason for the season! Even the long, cold, dark season of Winter. It's where we are tested, and where we learn hard lessons about trust and waiting even when sod all (well hello relevant gardening pun) seems to be happening!

Winter is temporary. If we endure it and have patience, the season will change and we will eventually see our seeds growing into dock off sequoias. Harvest will come.

What are we learning on the way to the fulfilment of our dreams? What kind of person are we growing into? Are we developing faith, trust, a strong character, hope and joy even when everything appears to be dark and disappointing?

If you feel like you are in the bleak mid-ruddy-winter, take heart! The harvest is coming, and there is plenty to learn along the way.

Most of our lives are lived in the middle of process. Throughout most of our lives we are waiting for something or other. It's so important that we learn to wait well and learn what we can in each season. I have not grasped this yet, but I'm really trying to. I want to keep dreaming big 'dock off sequoia' dreams, but also learn how to enjoy life in the process of getting there. It's a real skill to be able to dream big for the future, yet live fully in the here and now, and to believe in faith that the tiny seed will bear incredible sequoia-sized fruit in God's timing.

YNWA - Sum up and Reflect:

One other thing about sequoia trees is that they grow so big and strong because of the way their roots grow together with other sequoias. Their roots don't go down massively deep, but they intertwine with other sequoia tree roots and they grow together in groves. We don't need to do Winter - or any season - alone. We were made to grow tall dock off sequoias which stand together, not to stand in isolation. We should stand with others in difficult seasons, and celebrate with others at harvest time.

Who are you asking and receiving support from during your Winter season?

Who could you celebrate with today?

Who are you standing with through a difficult situation?

Prayer:

God, I admit that I really struggle during long Winter seasons. Things feel so bleak and like they will never change. God, today I'm so thankful for the way you chose to save us. You sent Jesus to earth to grow from a baby into an adult. You often work in slow ways, which can be hard for us to get on board with as we live in such a quick fix society. Please help me to develop patience and to live with a deep hope that the seeds of dreams in my heart will come to harvest, and, in your timing, will grow into sequoia-sized fruit. Help me to trust that this season will shift, and help me to learn all I need to right where I currently am. Amen.

16th DECEMBER – ALL GOOD IN THE OODIE?

2 Corinthians 3:18 - "But we all with unveiled faces, beholding and reflecting like a mirror the glory of the Lord, are being transformed into the same image from glory to glory, even as from the Lord's spirit."

This Winter I have treated myself to an 'oodie' (OK, it was a fake, cheaper Amazon version of an actual bonafide 'oodie'). An oodie is a huge wearable blanket with a hood, and it's a thing of pure wonder and beauty. It's so cosy and snuggly! They come in a variety of colours and wacky patterns, such as covered in avocados and rubber ducks. Mine is a plain but *very* bright pink (faux) oodie.

I was snuggled up with my daughter in my non-oodie a couple of weeks ago and I was concerned about her as she looked very pink. She didn't appear to be ill at all, but when the colour didn't leave her face in a few hours I administered some Calpol.

The next evening she was the same funny colour again. As I was tempted to reach for the Calpol bottle again it suddenly dawned on me that her pink face was a result of the bright pink glow my neon pink oodie was emitting!! Epic parent fail - administering an unnecessary dose of Calpol when the real issue was a brightly coloured wearable blanket!!

I wonder what we are reflecting to those in close proximity to us? To reflect means to show, to express, or to be a sign of something. What are we being a sign of? I'm all for us being real and not faking hyper-positive vibes when that's not how we feel. But I believe we can still choose to reflect peace in the middle of panic, faith in the middle of fear, and love in the middle of life's trials.

I was not aware of what I was reflecting to my daughter in my ridiculous neon pink oodie blanket. We can all similarly be unaware of what our lives are reflecting. We can slip into habits that do not reflect the person we really want to be. I know I'm often guilty of being snappy, sarcastic, and having an increasingly short fuse. These are not behaviours I want to reflect, but left unchecked, it's easy to carry on in these unhealthy patterns and responses to those around us. In my ignorance of my neon reflection, I actually thought it was my daughter who had the problem, in that I thought her pinkness meant she was ill. In actual fact the problem was me and what I was reflecting onto her. This can be the case in our relationships: we can be ignorant of our own shortcomings (the bad attitudes, negativity, etc, that we are reflecting to those around us) and we can even be deluded and think it's actually the fault of other people, or it's their problem.

Let's take a step back and do some self-reflection, asking the Holy Spirit to gently illuminate the areas of our lives where we are not reflecting Jesus well. Let's be realistic and honest with ourselves about the areas of our lives that may not reflect the values we hold as a Christian. Let's recognise that we are all reflecting and being a sign of something. Let's decide to make what we reflect real and genuine, but also positive, hopeful, and loving. Let's ask God to make his face shine on us so we can be a reflection of his goodness and light.

"The Lord bless you and keep you: the Lord make his face shine on you and be gracious to you: the Lord turn his face towards you and give you peace." (Numbers 6:24-26.)

YNWA - Sum up and Reflect:

When we become a Christian we become members of a 'royal priesthood.' (1 Peter 2:9.) You are clothed in royal robes that outshine any neon pink fake oodie!

Let's search our hearts and ask ourselves what our lives are reflecting to those around us. It's likely to be a mix of both positives and negatives.

Celebrate the ways you feel you are reflecting Jesus well to those around you, and take any areas of challenge that come up on the chin. Choose to work on those things so your reflection of Jesus becomes stronger.

In Romans 13:14, Paul challenges us: "clothe yourselves with the Lord Jesus Christ." If we clothe ourselves with him, we will truly reflect him well to a world that really needs to see him more.

Prayer:

God, thank you for this reminder that I am always reflecting something to those around me. I really desire to reflect you well and to be a sign of your kindness and love. Help me today as I reflect on the ways I could improve my reflection of you! Let your face shine upon me today God, I want to reflect your love, goodness, and light in a powerful way. Amen.

17th DECEMBER – JINGLE BELLS (AND FIRE BELLS)

Proverbs 16:24 - "Kind words are like honey - sweet to the soul and healthy for the body."

I had to take my daughter for a hospital appointment this week and I was not looking forward to it, as I suspected it would involve a blood test. This never goes down well (to put it mildly), which is no surprise really… it must be very difficult for her to understand what on earth is going on as I hold her in a vice-like grip and a nurse jabs a needle into her arm.

We saw the consultant which was all good, and he confirmed we would need to stay for a blood test. We had forty minutes to wait until the bloods clinic opened, which I said was fine as they had a nice little play area and Mr Tumble was on the TV. Job's a good'un, I thought, and I thought very wrong. We stepped out of the consultant's office and the loudest fire alarm I've ever heard in my life sounded non-stop for around twenty minutes (which felt like twenty years). My daughter isn't normally too bothered by noise, but this was so unbelievably loud she completely lost it. She just cried and screamed at the top of her lungs. I could hardly keep hold of her, and I had two coats and two bags which I kept dropping while she writhed around in my arms like a small crocodile that was trying to avoid being captured. It was all very loud, awkward, and embarrassing. We were both extremely sweaty, red, and stressed. A kind nurse gave us a side room, but my girl would not calm down. I told the nurse we'd have to leave as she couldn't cope with the screechy ear-piercing alarm any longer. The second I stepped out of the door the ruddy alarm stopped, and so did my daughter's screaming fit, so I legged it back in with her to have the blood test.

When it was all over and done with, I called a taxi to take us home. I felt really drained. The taxi pulled up and we hopped in, both relieved to be headed home. My daughter sang *Jingle Bells* (almost as loud as the fire bell had sounded) all the way home. She has two singing styles, one is sweet and tuneful and the other is 'foghorn on legs.' She was pelting it out full fog-horn on legs style for the whole journey. "DASHING THROUGH THE SNOW..." all loud and lairy as if she'd had way too many drinks on a pub crawl. The taxi driver was very quiet (not that I would've heard him if he'd been chatting) and I wondered what on earth he was thinking. Maybe he'd had a busy day and the last thing he wanted was foghorn leghorn blasting out their Christmas playlist in his cab. When we pulled up at home he said 'Your daughter is a very happy and content little girl, you should be very proud of her.' I was taken aback and pleasantly surprised by his kind words and I said 'I'm very proud but I'm also well stocked up on paracetamol!'

I had experienced a very stressful situation that day, and his kind words really lifted me and helped me to feel more calm – happy, even.

Kind words matter. They can soothe and comfort people who are experiencing a whole host of difficult situations in life. Christmas can be joyful for some and painful for others, and we don't always know which a person is experiencing. Let's be determined to speak as many kind words as we can this festive season, especially if someone burns the roast potatoes and sets off the smoke alarm.

YNWA - Sum up and Reflect:

God gifts us with people who speak kind things to us, sometimes when we least expect it. It could be a friend, relative, or even a random taxi driver you're never likely to meet again.

Thank God today for the kind words spoken over you recently.

Make sure you remember to speak kind words to others, especially during this festive season when tensions can run even higher than normal.

Recognise the power that your words hold to bring life, comfort, healing, and hope to others who may be in 'alarming' situations.

Prayer:

God, I want my words to bring life, healing, and comfort. At this time of year, when tensions can run higher than normal, help me to be determined to look for those who need a kind and encouraging word. Let the words I speak be like honey, as it says in the scripture for today. I spend time thanking you now for any kind words and encouragement that have recently been spoken over me. I ask you to keep reminding me of the power that my words can have for good in another person's life. I want to speak things over people that come from your heart of kindness. Amen.

18th DECEMBER – E.L.F. – GET OFF MY SHELF

James 5:16 – "Confess your sins to each other and pray for each other so that you can live together whole and healed."

I came downstairs at 2:00am a few nights ago with my snotty little girl and saw a big spider on the fireplace. I do not like spiders. Way too many legs IMO. But I remained calm and trapped the eight-legged freak (ELF) under a tea light holder. I felt like Bear Grylls - for about two seconds.

It's still there though, days later, as I'm too scared to properly deal with it. If I keep it covered at least it's off my mind a bit. I can try and pretend it's not there. But the reality is that it very much is there, prowling around - with all of its chuffin' legs.

I was hoovering the landing the other day and knocked over a toothbrush holder that I'm ashamed to say has been over-turned concealing another ELF for approx. *six months*. I just haven't been able to face dealing with it properly. I feared it escaping and running wild and out of control. I pass it many times each day but just tried to ignore it, though I knew it was ridiculous and that I just needed to deal with it. I'd learnt to live with an ELF in my life.

I think ELFs can represent stuff in our lives we know we need to deal with but aren't facing up to. It could be many different things - financial problems, secret addictions, bad attitudes, relational struggles. We become aware of them and don't like them so we cover them and think 'I'll deal with that later. It's covered, it's contained, I'm aware of it and it's not doing any harm really.'

But covering stuff can lead to being in denial, and a refusal to deal with things does no good long-term. It can also lead to shame and fear. I keep nearly having a heart attack when my daughter went anywhere near the concealed ELF in case she let it loose. We can live in fear of others discovering whatever it is we are concealing or desperately trying to keep covered in our lives.

It's not wise to share your hidden ELFs with every man and his dog. But bringing them to light and sharing them with a couple of close and trusted people means you can properly deal with them. You *can* get them out of your home/your life for good. It will more than likely require time, maybe some tears, some hard work, some focused prayer - but you can get rid of them instead of living with them permanently concealed and taunting you from inside their cover. In *Frozen* they sing "conceal don't feel… let it go" but I'd argue in this case we need to reject this Frozenology and 'deal with, not conceal' and then we can *truly* let go of the hidden nasties. Let it go for good!

Being vulnerable about our struggles and weaknesses is really tough, but absolutely necessary if we want to live a life of freedom. Everyone on this planet has ELFs in their lives. We all need help from others to deal with them.

Tonight I'll be asking my husband to help me get rid of the ELF on the fireplace. He will put some card under the tea light holder, I will open the door and probably squeal a bit (a lot), he will pretend he's going to throw it at me (why does this have to happen every single time?) but together we will get rid of it.

What ELFs do you have in your inner life that you need to deal with? Deal with it - don't conceal it, and then *truly* let the little suckers go.

YNWA - Sum up and Reflect:

God wants us to be free from the ELFs that are prowling around with their many legs undercover in our lives. If we expose them and face up to them they really can be dealt with and chucked into the sea. (Micah 7:19.)

We are not supposed to deal with them on our own. God wants us to confess them to him, but also to share our hidden sins/fears/anxieties/struggles with other trusted Christians who can help us find true freedom from them.

What ELFs do you have in your inner life that you need to deal with and stop concealing? Deal with it, don't conceal it, and then *truly* let them go.

Who can you confess them to, so you can find lasting freedom and healing from them?

Prayer:

God, it's so uncomfortable discussing things in my life that I'm struggling with. It's easier just to cover them and delay dealing with them. But I know ultimately this is no good. I know I need to properly deal with these sins, issues and secret addictions so I can be truly free. Highlight someone to me today who I can confide in and receive godly wisdom from. Give me the desire to properly clear out these things. I want to live 'whole and healed' as your word says, so today I choose to bring into your light the things I've kept hidden in darkness for too long.

19th DECEMBER – LESSONS FROM WONKY VEGETABLES

Psalm 139:13-14 - "For you created my inmost being, you knit me together in my mother's womb. I praise you for I am fearfully and wonderfully made."

Do you have a wonky narrative? You may think that's a very personal question, but stick with me, there is a sensible point I promise!

I watched a programme called *A Special School* on BBC2 this week. It's about a school in Wales for students with special needs. One of the teachers said the following, and it really impacted me:

"We need to work on correcting what we call a wonky narrative. A lot of our children feel really bad about themselves because of previous experiences or trauma. They've described themselves as really bad people, people who don't deserve our help or our love and attention. Our aim is to change that opinion of themselves. We work really hard to make them realise that they are really important to us and they really matter."

I love this. What a great mission and calling this teacher and this school has. Helping these young people with special needs see how valued and important they are, and correcting their 'wonky' perceptions of themselves.

I believe that many of us, like these young students, also live with a wonky narrative. We struggle with low self-esteem, feeling like we don't have much to offer and aren't really important. Sometimes we are wonky in the other direction and think too highly of ourselves, but most people I've met tend towards the wonky way of not feeling good enough or struggling with low self-worth.

During this festive season as we shop for our Christmas veg and we see the 'wonky' range, let it serve as a reminder that we can be involved in the important work of correcting wonky narratives. We can encourage and build others up and help to straighten out their wonky perceptions of themselves. We can make other people stand taller and feel loved and valued by telling them the amazing qualities we see in them. We can offer hope that the past doesn't have to determine the future, and remind them that they are a unique and wonderful creation with loads of God given potential and gifting to be used in this world. Words of life and encouragement have incredible power to correct wonky thinking and attitudes.

We can also work on correcting the wonky narratives and lies we have believed about ourselves for years, that have perhaps held us back from reaching our full potential. Today I challenge you to work on your wonky!

Let's make it our mission in this Christmas season to be correctors of wonky narratives. There's a lot of fear and uncertainty in the world we live in, and more than ever I believe we need to help each other straighten out our wonky narratives.

When it comes to fruit and veg I think wonky is wonderful! I regularly buy Aldi wonky blueberries - they are delish in my porridge and great value. I may well include some wonky parsnips in my Christmas dinner. But when it comes to our narratives and our perceptions of ourselves and others, wonky needs straightening out with godly truth and encouragement.

YNWA - Sum up and Reflect:

You are not wonky, you are wonderful! God has gifted you with a unique personality and skill set to contribute to this world in a way only you can. Don't let a wonky narrative about yourself hold you back.

Take as many opportunities as you can during this festive season to straighten out the wonky narratives you see in others.

Ask God to show you the areas of your life you've labelled as wonky and potentially unusable. Ask him to speak his truth into this.

Read the whole of Psalm 139 and spend time reflecting on this incredible passage which shows how much God knows and cares for you.

#workonyourwonky!

Prayer:

God, I recognise that I often subscribe to a wonky narrative. I think this may be due to difficult things I've experienced, or perhaps sins and regrets that have made me feel I don't deserve your love and kindness. At times I admit that I do feel wonky and unworthy. Help me today to digest this truth from Psalm 139 that says I am far from wonky, I am actually fearfully and wonderfully made. Help me to be a corrector of the wonky narratives I see in others around me, and use me to speak your truth over those who seem downtrodden and who also at times feel wonky and unworthy. Amen.

20th DECEMBER – THE ONE-EYED VIRGIN

Luke 2:19 - "But Mary stored up all these things and pondered them in her heart."

I knitted a 'knitivity' for my sister-in-law and I've managed to get it safely posted to her in good time for Christmas. Unfortunately, one of Mary's eyes has popped off in transit. Hence the title of today's thought being 'the one-eyed virgin.'

I'm always amazed by Mary when I think about her role in the Christmas story. The way she responded to what God asked of her is incredible to me. She was willing to serve God in this extremely odd circumstance and was prepared to trust him whilst facing the inevitable judgement and odd looks from people who just didn't believe it all to be true. Let's face it, not even Jeremy Kyle or Jerry Springer have come across such an unusual situation. 'I'm pregnant but I'm a virgin - it's not my fiancées baby, it's God's baby.' Wow.

I personally really do believe this is true though, as bizarre as it sounds, that Mary divinely was the mother of God. Even if it's verging/virgin on impossible!

If you've never heard Pentatonix sing *Mary Did You Know?* you must watch it on YouTube - it's amazing! I'm always a bit miffed when I watch it as I know I'll never look as cool as them in a cave with a candle. Anyway, I'll get over it (maybe, or maybe I've been practising in the garage with a hairbrush and a tealight).

The song asks if Mary knew all of the things Jesus would grow up to do (walk on water, give sight to the blind, calm storms) and even if she knew he was the great 'I am.' After my knitivity photo today I think I finally know the answer to the question "Mary did you know?" Wait for it...

...she had no idea

...no eye dear. Major LOLs.

Seriously though, I wonder how much she did know. She knew and believed she was carrying the Messiah, the Son of God, as the angel told her this (Luke 1:35). But did she know all of the things Jesus would grow up and do? Probably not, but she will have watched in wonder as Jesus did them as his life unfolded before her eye(s).

I'm encouraging myself to try to 'watch in wonder,' like I believe Mary did as she watched Jesus grow up, when it comes to my own life. Instead of stressing and worrying about what will be, what will happen next, I want to live with a sense of wonder about what God might do in and through me. To be excited about the ways I may partner with him over the coming months/years? I want to wonder in a way that's fuelled by faith and hope and a sense of adventure. I think that's how Mary watched and waited as Jesus grew and began to do all of the amazing things the song says about him.

We, like Mary, often have no idea what's round the corner. I think developing a strong sense of wonder and anticipation can mean this is an exciting way to live. We can wonder in a positive, faith-filled way, or we can engage in worry-fuelled wonder. Wondering means to be curious, to desire to know something, or to doubt. Which way of wondering do you tend towards? For a lot of my life I think I've wondered in a way that's not particularly positive. I've more often wondered what's going to happen in quite a defeatist and doubting way, rather than an 'excited to see what happens' way.

I'm feeling really challenged to rediscover a way to wonder that's more in line with my faith and what the bible says. I'm not talking about a Disney-type style of wonder - staring wide eyed out of a castle window with birds helping me get dressed, wondering when Prince Charming will rock up (because he already did 18 years ago - happy with that Rod?!). I'm talking more about discovering a sense of wonder and excitement at what might happen next in my life. The bible says that God has planned good things in advance for us to do (Ephesians 2:10) and that nothing is impossible with God (Matthew 19:26). If all that is true, and I believe it is, then why would I live in a kind of wonder that's gloomy and negative?

Life is not always rosy. Sometimes it's extremely challenging. This year certainly has been for me. I'm not advocating an annoyingly sickly sense of starry-eyed wonder that everything will always be dreamy and amazing. But sometimes I think we need to shift our perspective as we wonder. When we reflect on the wonders God has done, it helps us to wonder well for our own lives. Another definition of wonder is "a feeling of amazement and admiration, caused by something beautiful, remarkable or unfamiliar." The bible is full of wonder and miracles - incredible things God did that are supernatural and seemingly impossible. He is a God of wonder! The Red Sea was parted, giants defeated, the walls of Jericho came down, water was turned to wine, Jesus walked on water and healed people from many different diseases. These are wonders we need to reflect on as we wonder about our own circumstances.

This type of wonder will fuel our faith in our incredible wonder working God.

YNWA - Sum up and Reflect:

When you wonder in fear and doubt it leads to negative thinking, apprehension, and gloom about the future. When you wonder with faith and expectation and a focus on the amazing things God has done, it leads to optimism, excitement, and a sense of being involved in an adventure, where who knows what might happen.

I know which form of wonder I'm going to be working on! Let's be people who wonder well, like I believe Mary did.

Which way of wondering are you currently leaning towards?

Write down a wonder list - make a list of as many incredible and wonderful things you can think of - from the bible, from your own life and from the lives of other believers. Reflect on your wonder list and let this fuel you with faith-filled wonder as you go forward. Maybe you could create your own 'Wonderwall' at home? God bless the Gallagher brothers for inspiring that thought.

Prayer:

God, I want to be a person who wonders well. I want to set aside the negative, fear driven, doubt-filled wonder I'm prone to engaging in. I long to wonder in a way that is faith-fuelled, that recognises your awesome power and reflects on the wonders you have performed. Thank you for the wonder found in the Christmas story. Thank you for the many biblical characters who watched in wonder as the story of your son Jesus unfolded. I also want to learn to watch in wonder. To learn to align myself with the incredible potential each day that I walk with you holds. Help me to wonder well. Amen.

21St DECEMBER –
CERTIFICATES AND TICKETS

Ephesians 4:2 – "Be completely humble and gentle; be patient, bearing with one another in love."

Yesterday morning two things arrived in the post. One made my heart happy and one made my heart sink. One was my certificate for passing a course in British Sign Language. Great news to mark a lot of hard work. The other was a speeding ticket. Bad news of an expensive mistake. Highs and lows all in the space of two minutes.

It would've been nice to have received these items on different days as the ticket detracted a bit from the certificate. But it reminded me that life is made up of both moments - moments of certificates and moments of speeding tickets. Good news and bad news. Celebration and commiseration. Achievement and failure. Some days are full of joy, some full of sadness or disappointment and some, like yesterday, a weird combination of both.

It also made me think about how we don't always know whether another person is having a certificate or a ticket day - or like me a combo of both - a 'certicketficate' day if you will! (try saying that after a couple of Christmas sherries).

Some people we meet are currently having a 'certificate' experience of life. Maybe they have a job they love, they are in a happy relationship, have enough money in the bank and some interesting hobbies. They love Christmas and are excited about spending the next week or so catching up with friends and family for festive fun.

Other people we meet may be in more of a 'ticket' time. Days mixed with anxiety, struggle, sickness, bereavement, unemployment, redundancy, loneliness, and stress. The pressure of the next couple of weeks gives them high levels of anxiety as they have to endure Christmas parties and festive gatherings which they just don't feel like going to.

Some, like me, are having a 'certicketficate' experience. Some struggles and very challenging moments alongside some moments of real peace and joy despite what's going on in life.

We often don't quite know where others are at. In our uncertain world we need love, grace, and understanding. All of us will experience the certificate moments and the ticket moments in life, but we don't hit these in sync with each other. You might be having a certificate day, but your spouse, neighbour, or colleague may be in ticket mode. We need to be loving and sensitive in relation to where other people might be at, especially at Christmas time when emotions can be heightened.

Let's celebrate with each other in the certificate moments, console each other in the ticket moments, and understand that people's faces in certicketficate moments may look a bit weird - it's hard for one's chops to express this odd combo of feelings. Let's recognise that our situations are not all the same and that at any given moment we are all swinging between these different feelings and emotions. We often don't know the depth of the battles each other are facing, so let's be as kind and understanding as we can.

YNWA - Sum up and Reflect:

Life for all of us is full of ups and downs. Christmas can be a massively happy time for some and a shockingly difficult time for others. It can also be a weird mixture of joy and sorrow consecutively.

Let's do our best to extend grace and kindness to each person we meet, recognising that they may be going through a tough time. Let's be gentle with ourselves and others through ticket times. And let's celebrate ourselves and others in certificate times. Overall, let's be sensitive as we often don't know if it's a ticket, certificate or certicketficate day.

Are you experiencing a certificate day or a ticket day - or a mix of both? Bring your highs and lows to God in prayer now.

Think of someone you know for whom Christmas will be a challenging time. Spend some time in prayer for them, and let them know they've been on your heart and mind. Ask God for a specific scripture to share with them.

Prayer:

God, I want to be a person who is sensitive to the people around me. I want to love and support others really well. Help me to celebrate with those I meet who are in certificate mode and to show empathy and concern to those who feel they've been handed a ticket. Life is such a mixed bag of emotions, help me to be kind to myself and to others this Christmas, as we navigate what can be both a challenging and joyful season.

22nd DECEMBER – FESTIVE FOIBLES

1 Peter 4:8 - "Let us love one another for love covers a multitude of sins." [and peeves]

Anyone else noticed that the little things about others that get on your nerves seem to be heightened in holiday seasons? My pet peeves include wet towels left on our bed, cupboards and drawer doors being left open, and mugs being left around and not returned to the kitchen. I've recently discovered a fresh new pet peeve as I appear to have stepped into a new role of 'the kitchen roll police.' Where's Juan Sheet off the kitchen roll advert when you need him?

We recently decided to buy paint for four rooms in our house and get them done while we had some extra time indoors. My husband had a week off and worked super hard getting it done. Three out of the four rooms are complete. Boom! Very productive, and our house is looking good.

However, the painting of our rooms led to me stumbling upon what I can only describe as gross kitchen roll misconduct. I found a paint lid in our kitchen that sat on not one, not two, but *three* sheets of kitchen roll. I came very close to losing my sheet so to speak. I later caught my hubby drying his hands with *two* sheets of the precious stuff the same day. When I see what I deem to be unacceptable sheet usage, my blood pressure rockets - I just cannot fathom this reckless behaviour. I'm sure you'll have your own pet peeves and can relate in some way. There are also many festive foibles at this time of year, including putting chocolate wrappers back in the tin, which should 100% result in time behind bars if you ask me - and I'm not referring to bars of Dairy Milk.

But while they can bring amusement, we do need to be careful with these peeves and foibles. Because they can blow up out of all proportion and make us irritable, grinchy, and ungracious. They can also make us forget all of the good the peeve perpetrator/festive foibler does. I'm peeved that three sheets have been wasted with a tin of paint stood on them. But in my 'peevage' I'm forgetting that the peeve perpetrator has taken a week off work and painted three rooms as he wants to improve our home and make it a lovely living space for us.

So today's thought is: 'don't permit your pet peeves to prevent a positive perspective on the peeve perpetrator.' Or 'forget focusing on festive foibles and find freedom and forgiveness for the forthcoming festivities.' Very short and snappy helpful little phrases I know, you are welcome - feel free to get them printed on a mug/T-shirt!

YNWA - Sum up and reflect:

We are all irritating at times, with weird little habits and annoying quirks. Let's try to 'peer beyond the peeves' and 'focus beyond the festive foibles' and remind ourselves of the good stuff about each other. Let's remind each other of this good stuff too - letting someone know what we appreciate about them robs the peeve of its power. Love covers a multitude of peeves.

Who is really irritating you right now, or who does the thought of spending time with over the festive season fill you with dread? Be honest with God about this, and ask him for bucket loads of grace with this person. Ask him to highlight the good qualities in them too, and thank him for those.

NB - as the advert rightly stated - "Juan sheet does plenty."

Prayer:

God, as I spend more concentrated time with family and friends this festive season, I pray that you'll help me to keep the peeves in perspective. I acknowledge that I have strange little quirks that must irritate other people, as much as their weird little ways can wind me up. Help me to see all of the good qualities in those around me, and to elevate those above the peeves I hold. As I do my best to love and appreciate people, please give me divine help to peer beyond the peeves, and remind me to tell people the things they do and qualities they have that I really appreciate. Amen.

23rd DECEMBER – SLEIGH THE DAY

Galatians 6:9 - "Let us not become weary in doing good, for at the proper time you will reap a harvest if you do not give up."

In the run up to Christmas, my husband and I started a '90 day slay/sleigh' back in September. If we stick to our calorie target and exercise goal each day we get rewarded with a sticker on our chart, and if not we get a cross.

I did this because I heard a personal trainer saying that you might think you are very consistent, but unless you monitor it (he suggested for 90 days), you won't really know. If you are consistent at least 80% of the time you'll likely see results. If you stick to it less than that you won't see the results you desire.

I decided to monitor my consistency as I felt I was very consistent, yet not seeing the results I wanted. My 90 day sleigh chart demonstrates that I'm not nearly as consistent as I'd like to think I am, and it clearly shows why I'm not achieving my weight loss goals. I have bursts of doing well, but also bursts of losing the plot. There is wiggle room for not being on form every day. Like the trainer said, it's important that you stick to your plan 80% of the time. Life happens to us all, and there are times when we can't fulfil our intentions of consistency with our plan. But overall, being consistent most of the time is key to success.

Consistency means "steadfast adherence to the same principles, courses, form."

Or,

"The quality of always behaving or performing in a similar way."

We need to recognise the power of consistency in our lives. I personally think it's one of the most undervalued qualities ever. I think it's because there's no 'razzle dazzle' with it. It's found in making good choices in the daily grind, with no spotlight. It's often boring and hard work, and doing things that are tough but necessary to achieve your goals.

I think it's even harder to stay steady and consistent at Christmas time in many different aspects of our lives. In terms of our health - when life is different to the norm and motivation is low it's even more tempting to ditch the workout and shovel in the biscuits. I'm normally fairly well motivated to be healthy and exercise, but I'm now in full-on festive mode, wanting to drink copious amounts of hot choc and mulled wine and stuff my chops with Lindt balls. The dark mornings make me more sleepy and less inclined to 'wake up and work out.' But if I let all of my consistency go now, I'll end this year frustrated that I've undone a lot of hard work and discipline. There's the 20% wiggle room to enjoy festive treats which I'm all up for, but I can't just resign myself to burying my snout in the Quality Street tin - as appealing as that sounds!

I tried to think of an example of a biblical character who displayed consistency and I had a total mind blank, so of course I Googled it! Daniel came up as a man who displayed consistency. As I read up on this, I realised how true this was. Daniel prayed three times a day, it was a consistent habit that helped him to stay connected to God. When King Darius created a new law whereby prayer (to any god or human other than the King) was banned, Daniel consistently cracked on with his thrice a day prayer sessions, undeterred by the new law. The King was actually a big fan of Daniel, he had really been tricked into enforcing the prayer ban by leaders who wanted rid of Daniel. The punishment Daniel faced for consistently praying as he always had was being thrown into the lions' den. King Darius says to Daniel: "May your God, *whom you serve continually,* rescue you!" (Daniel 6:16.) And God certainly did save Daniel from the lions' mouths - what a 'roarsome' miracle!

I would love to be so consistent that people recognise I continually serve God, as Daniel did. In honesty, I am nowhere near as consistent as I should be or want to be. As I write this today I'm using this 'God prod' I'm feeling as an opportunity to assess my habits and my daily practices, particularly in spiritual terms. How can I be more consistent in prayer, in loving others, in serving God? I really desire to be a consistent person, but often I'm so busy and distracted that the most important things go out the window. I do pray, but often it's very self-focused and 'emergency' style prayers, rather than deliberate and considered time set aside to pray for myself and for others.

We can look at people who achieve their goals and dreams and imagine they are a bit jammy and have stumbled on success. Or we can look up to other believers who we admire and think God just made them more spiritual than we are. But more often than not, they have done the daily grind - those small consistent acts that have eventually got them to their place of success and to attaining what they set out to do.

Commit to being a person who is consistent. It may not be the most exciting thing to do, but the results of being consistent on a daily basis can really pay off in the long run. Consistency is key to sleigh/slay each day.

YNWA - Sum up and Reflect:

If you, like me, are struggling to stay consistent in an area of your life, take some time to embrace the 'God prod' and re-assess things today.

Are your spiritual disciplines in place and helping you to 'serve God continually' as Daniel did?

What daily practices do you need to begin, or be consistent in to ensure your spiritual life is flourishing? Is there anything you used to do regularly that, due to the busyness of life, you have let slip?

Write down your goals and some daily consistent steps you can take to get there.

If it floats your boat, get a habit tracker app or do some kind of visual chart to measure your progress and track your consistency.

Prayer:

God, I desire to be a consistent person. I want to develop disciplines that help me to have a successful life, where I can reach my full potential and bless and serve you and others. I'm sorry that so often I get distracted in the busyness of life and I neglect the important things such as regular prayer, studying your word and spending time listening to you. Help me as I set some goals today relating to increasing my consistency. I acknowledge that you reward consistent behaviour, and that in Daniel's story, you did an incredible miracle in protecting him from the mouths of the lions sent to devour him. As this year soon draws to a close and I consider my hopes and dreams for the next year, help me to make consistency a priority and help me to think of practical steps I can take towards becoming a consistent person. Amen.

Recommended reading: *Atomic Habits* by James Clear

24th DECEMBER – THE MOST WONDERFUL TIME OF THE YEAR?

2 Corinthians 12:9-10 - "But he said to me, "My grace is sufficient for you, for my power is made perfect in weakness. Therefore I will boast all the more gladly about my weaknesses, so that Christ's power may rest on me....For when I am weak, then I am strong."

I am a big fan of Christmas. I love the twinkly lights, the festive treats, the get-togethers with friends and family, and special services at church. It feels like such a lovely time where people are in good spirits and life just feels a bit more magical.

But this morning, on Christmas Eve, I have to admit that I reached a breaking point. This has not happened to me in this way before, especially at this time of year as I love it so much.

Our little girl has been ill now for the last six weeks. Nothing serious thankfully, but a string of coughs and colds that seem to return about an hour after we thought they'd gone. Each one brings snot-filled days and cough-filled nights. She has not slept through in weeks, and we've had many nights with just a couple of hours sleep. I started a new job two months ago and I am working quite a few more hours each week, and this has been tricky as I've had to go in feeling like a zombie on quite a few occasions due to the lack of sleep. Not ideal when you are trying to make a good impression and you feel like the walking dead!

It was my turn to have a proper sleep last night, but our girl was awake coughing solidly from 3:00-6:00am and sleeping through it was impossible. I went downstairs and broke down in tears to my husband. I have reached the point where I just cannot be bothered with Christmas. I don't want it to happen. I don't want to clean, cook, and talk to people, even people I really love. I want to curl up in a ball and hibernate for a few weeks. The backlog of so little sleep has really caught up with me and I feel like I've nothing left to give. I just want to sleep. Like Mariah Carey, I don't want a lot for Christmas, there is just one thing I need - some flippin' undisturbed shut eye (don't think that's quite what Mariah had in mind, but it most definitely is what I want!).

I have felt very angry at God during this prolonged period of disturbed nights. I have prayed so hard for my girl to get better, and I know in an instant God could help her and stop this constant string of viruses attacking her body and hijacking our sleep. The fact that he hasn't makes me really mad. I believe he is powerful and more than able to change this situation for us. Yet he hasn't, and that makes me angry. It makes me feel like prayer is pointless, not just for myself but for others who are in difficult situations. If I'm not experiencing him intervening in my difficult times, how can I have faith to pray for others?

As I have prayed, the verse that has kept buzzing through my mind is "my grace is sufficient for you, for my power is made perfect in your weakness." (2 Corinthians 12:9.) This really cheeses me off, as I feel that God is saying he may not take this trial away, but he will show his power through the weakness, exhaustion, and vulnerability I currently feel. Not really the answer I want, I'd prefer the instant healing thank you kindly. That scripture was in my head again yesterday, as I picked up a book I've been reading. The next chapter was about leading through weakness and vulnerability. Guess what the key scripture was?! The author also talked about embracing the gift of your 'limp,' whatever that may be for you. He even gave some suggestions, one being caring for a child with special needs, which was very specific for me.*

So the gift I am going to try to be thankful for this Christmas is an unexpected one. It's the gift of weakness. The gift of God showing his power through my life when I feel at my worst. When I feel like I have nothing good left in me and when I've prayed angry sweary prayers that I feel embarrassed by. When I feel a lack of hope and enthusiasm for life, even when it's the most wonderful time of the year. Yes I feel weak and vulnerable, but I have to trust that his grace will be sufficient to get me through this challenge. The scripture goes on to say that when I am weak, it's then that I am actually strong. So unlike Elton John, I won't be stepping into Christmas this year, I'll be limping, but that is more than OK. Keep calm and limp on!

YNWA - Sum up and Reflect:

We all have different areas of vulnerability, limitation, and weakness. These things don't magically disappear at Christmas, and the expectation and pressure for us to be festive and chirpy can be way too much! Try to hold on to the truth that His grace is enough for you. Embrace the gift of your weakness and allow God to use it as a vehicle to show his great power.

Is there an area of your life where you feel particularly weak at the moment?

What would you consider your 'limp' to be?

Ask God to use you 'limp and all' this festive season, and embrace the truth that when you feel weak, that's the perfect opportunity for God to show his power through your life.

Remember that when you are limping, crutches are an aid. If you need to reach out for support then go for it, we all experience times when we need help, be it emotional, physical, spiritual, or practical.

Consider what kind of crutch/help you may benefit from in regards to your limp - and be bold enough to reach out to someone and ask for it.

Prayer:

God, in all honesty, the challenges of life can feel all too much. Sometimes I feel at breaking point and I don't feel much hope or joy, even during 'the most wonderful time of the year.' Thank you for the wisdom gleaned from the emotionally healthy material about embracing the gift of my weakness and my limp. I am so longing for you to show your power through my weakness and vulnerability. Give me strength to face this day and to take confidence that when I am weak, your strength can most powerfully be at work within me. Amen.

Emotionally Healthy Discipleship by Pete Scazzero, p187-209 (2021, Zondervan Reflective)

25th DECEMBER – TURKEY TERROR

Ephesians 5:1-2 - "Follow God's example, therefore, as dearly loved children and walk in the way of love…"

Ok, so 'Turkey terror' may be a bit of a seasonal exaggeration, but we did have a moment of pretty intense poultry related panic a few nights ago. We had ordered our Christmas bird from Iceland (don't turn your nose up, they've won a few 'Good Housekeeping' awards I'll have you know). I said to my husband a few evenings ago, "do we need to check about when we defrost the bird"? (Why do we refer to it as 'the bird' but only at Christmas? Any other time of year we'd just say the chicken or the turkey, but at Christmas for some reason it's formally referred to as 'the bird'.) Anyway, we agreed it was a good idea and went to check the instructions on 'the bird's' packaging. To our horror it instructed us to leave the all-important bird in the fridge to defrost for *ninety six hours* before the big day. I think we worked out we had around sixty hours until we needed it to go in the oven. Our giblets were officially in a twist, our tinsel was well and truly in a tangle. After a few moments of mild panic (which was largely just me remembering the episode of *The Royle Family* where they are attempting to defrost their turkey in a bath with a hairdryer) I took a deep breath, looked at the instructions again, and realised one option listed was to cook it from frozen. Bang it in the oven for 4.5

hours from frozen and job's a good'un. Phew. Turkey terror can leave, it's all good in the poultry hood thanks to the packaging advice: :for best results cook from frozen.:

Freezing is such a helpful function, in this case, as a way of storing food. It preserves food and means it can last longer, and in some cases, like with our festive bird, it makes it an easier and quicker option for cooking.

In life, however, if we are not careful we can stay locked in a frozen internal world. The definition of 'frozen' along with its positive links to food preservation can also mean "incapable of being changed, moved, or undone." It's linked to something being fixed and immovable. If someone stands very still it can be said that they are 'frozen to the spot,' or people can be so scared that they are described as being 'frozen with fear.'

The state of being frozen can be very limiting in our lives. Sometimes being frozen is caused by huge life altering events like abuse, grief, and loss, and that's not what I am referring to here, as I don't for a minute want to underplay the seriousness and impact these things can have on people's lives and the professional help that is needed. You can't just 'defrost' in a few hours and return to normal after these experiences. I really believe in the power of therapy and taking the time to heal properly.

What I'm referring to in my reflection today are the things that affect us all in life, that may not be huge or life-altering on their own, but that can accumulate and, if we are not careful, leave us a little more frozen each time. Frozen in fear, frozen in the past, frozen in self-preservation. It could be a hurtful comment, a failure of some kind, something we have said or done that we regret. Perhaps nothing huge on its own, but if not dealt with, and when added to other failures, mistakes, and hurts, can leave us increasingly frozen. We retreat a bit more, we lose a bit more confidence, we don't step out and take a risk on a new venture as we remember how we failed last time.

Sometimes I get a flashback of something I've done or said, even from years ago. It can be something I know I've asked God for forgiveness for, but it wants to bite me in the butt and leave me frozen in my failure and shortcomings. I'm learning to use the power of freezing back in these situations. 'Fight fire with fire' they say, but I say 'fight frozen with frozen!' If you've ever had a verruca (what a lovely festive topic!) you may know that there was a treatment where they froze them off - they literally jabbed it with a big ice poker thing with liquid nitrogen on the end and froze the little sucker as many times as it took to get rid of it. I think we need a similar approach when these thoughts/memories/negative experiences come to try and freeze us in fear and failure. Like a verruca, these negative thoughts can become beliefs and grow deep and take root in our lives. We need to be feisty and freeze them in their tracks straight away. Replace the negative, fear driven, thoughts with God's perspective. 'You are a failure, you will always fail' could be replaced with 'I have failed in life, but I am deeply loved by God and I'm moving forward in faith - I am loved and I am forgiven.' 'I wish I'd never said that' could be replaced with 'I've said some stupid things, but today is a clean slate and I'm determined that my words from now on will bring life and love.' Jab and freeze the suckers with God's truth until they do one, and they'll crumble away as a verruca does when up against the ice poker!

So use freezing for good – use it to fight the negative recurring thoughts and regrets that try to leave you frozen in fear and helplessness. But in terms of our hearts, let's keep them warm and 'thawed to the Lord' if you will! Warm, soft, and tender hearts will be a great aid for us to 'walk in the way of love.' You can walk in the way of love much more effectively with verruca-free trotters :)

#thawedtotheLord

YNWA - Sum up and Reflect:

Christmas is a time when we reflect on Immanuel, God with us. We celebrate that Jesus was born and entered into our brokenness and humanity. He knows we all fail and fall, and he wants to bring us freedom from the frosty fear we can become paralysed by. He wants to free us from the regrets and mistakes of the past that try to leave us frozen solid.

Allow his great love to thaw the frosty areas of your heart and mind, and go forward with confidence knowing that unlike our turkey, you are not best served from frozen. Defrost yourself thoroughly so you can be used to your best potential in the year ahead.

What are the recurring thoughts and memories that can leave you feeling discouraged and frozen?

What recent experiences have affected your heart and left you a bit more frosty?

Spend some time with God now, thanking him for Jesus - Immanuel - God with us - who came to free us from all frosty fear and regret.

In what ways can you adjust your life and your attitude so you can 'walk in the way of love' rather than being frozen to the spot in fear?

Prayer:

God, I thank you for this special day - thank you that today I can celebrate because you came down. You are Immanuel - God with us - and you are with us through the highest of highs and the lowest of lows. Thank you that in all of my failures and the things I regret, you stand by me - you take the burden of sin from my shoulders. Help me to recognise thoughts that are recurring and that leave me frozen in fear or frozen to the spot and prevent me from moving forward in my faith journey. Help me to 'defrost' today, as I reflect on your perfect and unending love for me, let my heart be thawed for you Lord. I want to 'walk in the way of love' so that others can see your love shine through me. Help me to have a thankful, soft, and warm heart. Amen.

P.S. I hope the mention of verrucas doesn't put you off your festive feast today!

ABOUT THE AUTHOR

Kate lives in Yorkshire with her magician husband Rod and her sassy seven year old daughter Chloe, who rocks her extra chromosome.

Kate is passionate about writing and speaking, and aims to bring the truth of the bible to life in a relevant and real way. She is unashamed about her love for terrible jokes and puns which are sprinkled throughout her writing.

She is in her happy place when she's in a coffee shop, writing away with a one shot latte and a caramel shortbread.

This is Kate's second book, and if you enjoyed it you can check out her first book, *When God 'Buts' In* - available on Amazon.

Kate writes devotional plans for the YouVersion Bible app. You can search for the following plans on there: 'Sling it – Standing Strong in Giant-sized battles,' 'Control Freak,' and 'The Sky's the Limit, Innit?'.

Kate enjoys speaking - if you want to book her to speak at your church or group please get in touch – details below.

Connect with Kate:
Email: katewilliamswriting@gmail.com
Instagram: @katewilliamswrites
Facebook: Kate Williams

Printed in Dunstable, United Kingdom